Microsoft Word
For Beginners

By Web Wise Seniors, Inc.
An Educational Organization for Beginning Computer Users

Web Wise Seniors, Inc.
305 Woodstock Rd.
Eastlake, Ohio 44095
www.WebWiseSeniors.com

I

Copyright

Trademarks

Windows is a registered trademark of Microsoft. All other brand names and product names used in this book are trademarks, registered trademarks, or trade names of their respective holders. Web Wise Seniors (WWS) is not associated with Microsoft or any other product or vendor mentioned in this book.

Limits of Liability/Disclaimer or Warranty

Sales Inquiries

For sales inquiries and special prices for bulk quantities, please call toll free (866) 232-7032.

Introduction

"The best computer class I have ever taken!" and "I never knew that computers could be explained so well!" are comments heard frequently from Web Wise Senior students. Since 2000, Web Wise Seniors has successfully taught thousands of beginning computer users. Now, for the first time, the same teaching methods successful in Web Wise Seniors' courses are found in this easy to understand book.

This book is not a reference for Microsoft Word. It is a learning guide for people of any age who are unfamiliar with the Microsoft Word program, but is especially designed for seniors who want to be skilled word processors. It is like having a private instructor at your side as you walk through the basics of word processing with your book. It is full of common questions asked by beginners in actual classes, followed by easy to understand answers that have already helped thousands.

You only get so far by reading explanations and definitions. You need to actually use Microsoft Word to learn to use it well. This book will help you do just that. It will help you get started using Microsoft Word by walking you through the basic skills step-by-step while answering your "whys" and "whats" along the way.

Web Wise Seniors teaches basic computer classes every day. WWS instructors have seen firsthand what works, what doesn't work, and what beginners want to know. We have draw on their knowledge, skills, and experience to write this book.

About the Authors

Web Wise Seniors is a company dedicated to teaching basic computer skills to individuals over the age of 50. Since 2000, Web Wise Seniors has filled over 25,000 classroom seats throughout Ohio and Pennsylvania, and has quickly become a premier computer education company for mature adults in the Midwest.

Classes have been designed for seniors by seniors and continually updated with the feedback of its students. By becoming an interactive part of the senior community and working closely with senior organizations throughout the Midwest, Web Wise Seniors has been able to develop a unique teaching style and curriculum that have been overwhelmingly successful.

Since 2000, over 97% of Web Wise Seniors students have stated they would recommend the program to their friends and family. 100% of affiliated teaching locations have been happy to work with the WWS program and, out of a 4 point scale, WWS received on average a 3.8 rating in student satisfaction.*

The same dedication and love of teaching that has made the WWS program so successful in the classroom is available for you in the pages of this book. Readers will find this book full of examples, illustrations, and easy to follow directions. This is a teaching guide, not just a manual or reference book.

*Student satisfaction as collected through WWS classes and events (2000 – 2008).

About this Book

Microsoft Word for Beginners is designed to be read in order. Readers should begin with page one and continue through the book as if they were actually taking a computer course. The sections all relate and build upon each other.

Readers should keep a computer close at hand while reading *Microsoft Word for Beginners*. We recommend you read through an entire section and then go back and try the steps outlined in the section.

Keep a pen or pencil handy too. Take notes and highlight any sections that you feel are personally important. This is your computer book and the more personal references you make within its pages, the better this course will work for you.

Above all, please enjoy *Microsoft Word for Beginners*. Read at your own pace and keep at it. You'll be a word processing wiz before you know it!

Meet Larry

Larry is the Web Wise Seniors mascot. He will be found throughout the pages of this book, helping you to "get the bugs out". Larry has been helping beginning computer users for over two years now. He runs the Web Wise Seniors help desk on www.WebWiseSeniors.com and often makes guest appearances in WWS publications.

In his spare time, Larry enjoys searching the Internet, e-mailing friends, and belly dancing.

Acknowledgements

We would like to thank the thousands of students that have challenged our computer instructors' minds in class. Your countless, and sometimes off-the-wall, questions and constructive feedback have made us better teachers. Without you, this book would not have been possible. Thank you!

We would also like to thank our family members for their insight, feedback, and support.

Credits

Authors
Michael Douglas
Stephen Pelton

Book Design and Production
Michael Douglas
Stephen Pelton

Proof Reading
Jean Pelton
Mary Pelton

Clip Art
Microsoft 2003 Clip Art Gallery

Screen Shots
Microsoft Windows Vista

Table of Contents

Chapter 1: Let's Get Started

Table of Contents

Chapter 2: Formatting Fundamentals

Table of Contents

Chapter 3: Saving, Opening, and Closing

Table of Contents

Chapter 4: Aligning your Text

Chapter 5: Spelling and Grammar

Chapter 6: Printing a Document

Table of Contents

Chapter 7: Creating a New File

Chapter 8: Bullets and Numbers

Table of Contents

Table of Contents

Chapter 9: Page Borders

Chapter 10: Copying, Cutting & Pasting

Chapter 11: Saving Your Work to a Flash Drive

Table of Contents

Chapter 12: Shortcuts

Chapter 13: Addressing Envelopes

Table of Contents

Chapter 14: Page Layout and Margins

Chapter 15: Working with Pictures

Table of Contents

Chapter 16: Columns

Table of Contents

Chapter 1

Let's Get Started!

What You Will Learn in this Chapter
- ✓ Why Microsoft Word?
- ✓ Opening Microsoft Word
- ✓ Activating Microsoft Word
- ✓ Using tabs and ribbons
- ✓ The options located on the different ribbons
- ✓ The functions of important keyboard keys

Chapter 1: Let's Get Started!

Section 1: An Introduction to Microsoft Word

What is Microsoft Word?

Microsoft Word is the most popular word processing program used in business today. Microsoft Word is used to create letters, fliers, resumes, newsletters, and other professional looking documents. Word processing programs, such as Microsoft Word, are very similar in their basic functions to typewriters. Both place letters and numbers on paper. It is Microsoft Word's ability to add style, pictures, columns, and other elements to a document giving it a professional and exciting appearance that makes Microsoft Word a superior product. Microsoft Word's ability to provide its users with thousands of special functions makes it stand out from other word processing programs. Some of the special features that make Microsoft Word so useful include spell check, grammar check, text alignment, picture editing, mail merge, and much more. Throughout this book, these topics will be explored and the features used in real life examples. So put away that piece of paper and hold on. You're about to enter the exciting world of Microsoft Word.

Starting Microsoft Word

Let's get started. You now know Microsoft Word offers many great features, but how do you access the program? The first step is to open the Start menu. The Start menu can be accessed through the START button in the lower left corner of the computer screen. The START button is a blue circle surrounding the Microsoft symbol which looks like a multi-colored flag. Move your mouse pointer so it is positioned on top of the START button, and click your left mouse button one time. The Start menu will appear in the lower left side of the screen. The Start menu contains the option ALL PROGRAMS which lists all the available programs on the computer. To display the list, position your mouse arrow directly on top of the ALL PROGRAMS option. The ALL

PROGRAMS option will become highlighted in blue. Click the left mouse button one time, and a list of programs will appear. There are so many programs on the computer that a scroll bar will be displayed on the right side of the programs list. Use the scroll bar to locate the option MICROSOFT OFFICE. A small yellow folder will be located on the left side of the option MICROSOFT OFFICE. The yellow folder symbol indicates there are more options located within the folder. Place the mouse arrow on top of the MICROSOFT OFFICE option, and click the left mouse button one time. A list of all the Microsoft Office programs will be displayed. MICROSOFT OFFICE WORD 2007 will be displayed in the new list, preceded by a blue W in a square symbol. When you place your mouse arrow on the MICROSOFT OFFICE WORD 2007 option, it will become highlighted in blue. Click your left mouse button. The menu will disappear, and the Microsoft Word program will be opened.

Starting Microsoft Office Word 2007: Step by Step Instructions:
1. **Click the START button to open the Start menu.**
2. **Click the ALL PROGRAMS option.**
3. **Use the scroll bar to locate the MICROSOFT OFFICE option.**
4. **Click the MICROSOFT OFFICE option.**
5. **Click the MICROSOFT OFFICE WORD 2007 option to start the program.**

Chapter 1: Let's Get Started!

Starting Microsoft Office Word 2007: A Visual Guide

**Step 1:
Click the
START button.**

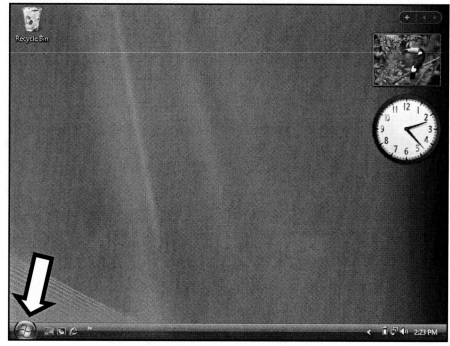

**Step 2:
Click ALL
PROGRAMS.**

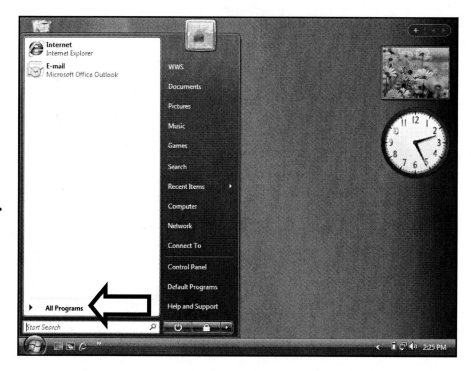

Step 3:
Use the scroll
bar to locate
MICROSOFT
OFFICE

Step 4:
Click
MICROSOFT
OFFICE

Step 5:
Click
MICROSOFT
OFFICE
WORD 2007

Chapter 1: Let's Get Started!

Section 2: Activating Microsoft Word

The Activation Process

The first time you open Microsoft Word, it will ask you to accept Microsoft's license agreement and to activate the program. The license agreement simply states that you will not make illegal copies of this program or use it for illegal activities. If you do not accept the agreement, Microsoft Word will automatically close, and you will not be able to use it. Click on the ACCEPT button to show you have read the agreement, accept the terms, and desire to continue to use the program.

After you have accepted the license agreement, Microsoft Word will automatically open an activation screen. The activation process can be completed over the Internet or via the telephone, but it must be completed. This is a copyright protection feature used by Microsoft to insure that only those people who have purchased the program can use it.

HINT: The easiest way to activate Microsoft Word is to make a brief phone call to Microsoft. A toll free phone number will be displayed on the activation screen after you select your country of residence.

Chapter 1: Let's Get Started!

Section 3: An Overview of Microsoft Word

Taking a Look at the Microsoft Word Screen

Microsoft Word is now open on your computer screen. Before you start typing, take a moment to look at its basic layout.

Located in the upper left corner of the Microsoft Word screen is a round gray circle adorned with the Microsoft symbol which consists of four multi-colored squares. This button is known as the OFFICE button. It provides access to a *list* of very important functions that will be discussed throughout this book.

The OFFICE button.

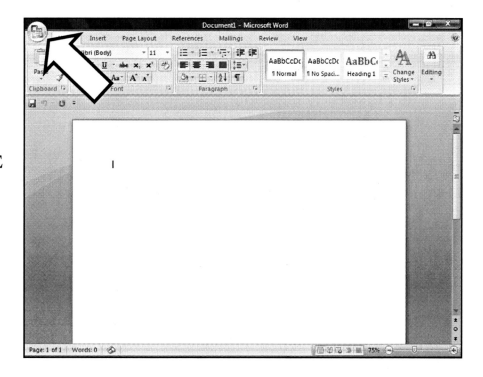

Chapter 1: Let's Get Started!

The Quick Access Toolbar will be displayed either to the right of the Office button of just below the ribbon on the left side of your screen. The Quick Access Toolbar, which works independently of the ribbon, contains the Save button, the Undo typing button, and the Repeat typing symbol (commonly called the Redo button). If you make an error, you can simply click the Undo button and your latest instruction to the computer will be undone. This incredibly useful button will be discussed in more detail later in this book.

The Quick Access toolbar.

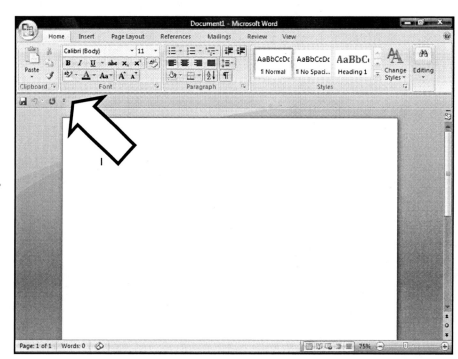

Look at the title bar of the program window. It is the black line at the top of your open screen/window. The title bar will read "Document1 – Microsoft Word." "Document1" is the generic name given to the blank piece of paper. If you open another new blank document, it will be given the name "Document2." Anything created using Microsoft Word is referred to as a document. When you save a document for the first time, the program will ask you to give it a new name. After the save process is complete, the name you chose will be displayed in the title bar of the window.

The minimize, maximize, and close buttons are located in the upper right corner of the screen. Now remember from our Basic Computer book, the minimize button has a minus sign on it. MINIMIZE removes the window from the screen, but does not close it. Your information is not lost. When you minimize a window, the window is stored on your task bar at the bottom of the screen. To retrieve your window, simply place your mouse arrow on top of the button on your task bar that represents the minimized window and press the left mouse button once. The window will return to the computer screen.

The MAXIMIZE button has one big square on it. When you press the maximize button, your window will stretch out to cover the entire computer screen. After a window has been maximized, the symbol on the maximize button changes. The one big square symbol turns into two small squares. This change occurs to tell you that you cannot make the window any larger. If you click the maximize button again, the window will be restored to its original, smaller, size.

The CLOSE button is located in the far right corner of each window. The close button has a big "X" on it. When you click on the close button, a message will appear asking you whether you want to save your changes. This is a good time to save your document. Saving is discussed in detail later in this book. If you click No, the document window will be removed from the computer screen, the window's button will be removed from the task bar, and unsaved information will be lost.

Minimize, Maximize, and Close buttons.

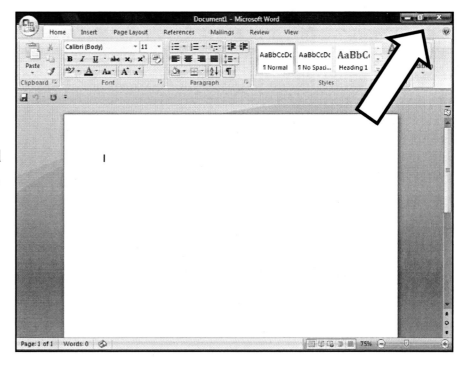

Chapter 1: Let's Get Started!

Located just below the title bar is the tab bar. The tab bar consists of seven different tabs; Home, Insert, Page Layout, References, Mailings, Review, and View. If you look just below the tab bar you will see an area filled with tiny symbols and pictures. These tiny symbols and pictures make up what is called the Ribbon. Each symbol on the ribbon represents a different function of Microsoft Word. As you can see, Microsoft Word has the ability to perform many different functions, the most useful of which will be discussed throughout this book.

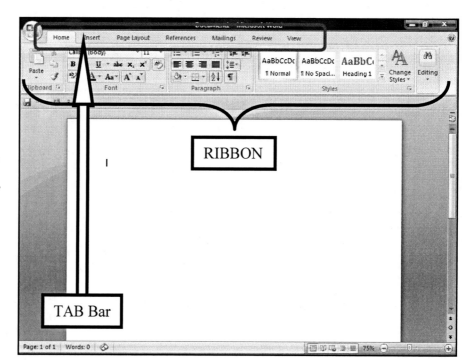

The TAB bar and RIBBON.

Overview of the Tabs and their Ribbons

The tab bar controls what symbols (functions) are displayed on the ribbon. If you place the mouse arrow on top of the Insert tab and click the left mouse button, a new set of symbols will be displayed on the ribbon. If you click on the Page Layout tab, another set of symbols will be displayed on the ribbon, and so on. In summary, the different tabs help categorize the numerous functions of Microsoft Word.

After opening any of the menus, position your mouse arrow over the desired option (picture). It will highlight in orange. To make the selection, click your left mouse button and the action will be performed.

Chapter 1: Let's Get Started!

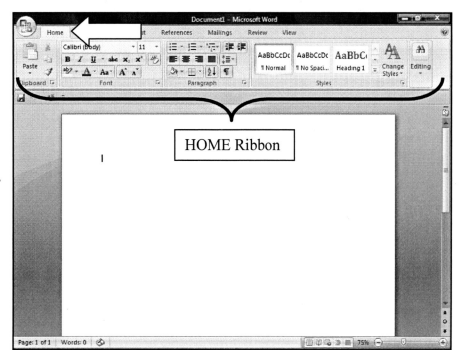

The HOME tab and ribbon.

HOME Ribbon

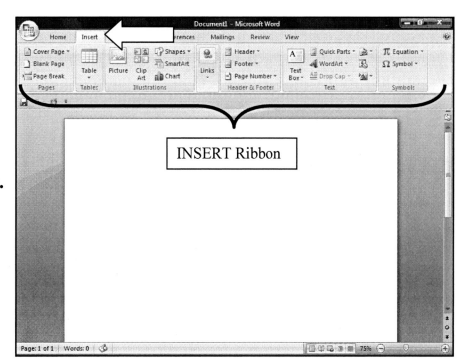

The INSERT tab and ribbon.

INSERT Ribbon

Chapter 1: Let's Get Started!

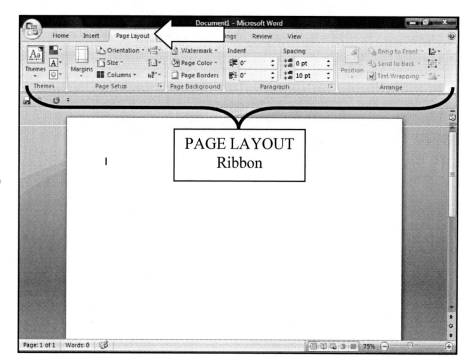

The PAGE LAYOUT tab and ribbon.

Using the Ribbons: Step by Step Instructions

1. Click on a tab, for example "Home."
2. Move the mouse arrow over the ribbon.
3. Place the mouse arrow on top of the desired option.
4. Click the left mouse button.

The following pages will summarize the tabs and the functions of their buttons.

Chapter 1: Let's Get Started!

Overview of the Home Tab
1. **Clipboard** – Cut, Copy, Paste, and Format Painter
2. **Font** – Select Text Style and Size, Bold, Italicize, Underline, Highlight Color, etc.
3. **Paragraph** – Bullets, Numbers, Alignment, Indent, Sort, etc.
4. **Styles** – Change the Set of Fonts, Styles, and Colors
5. **Editing** – Find, Replace, and Select

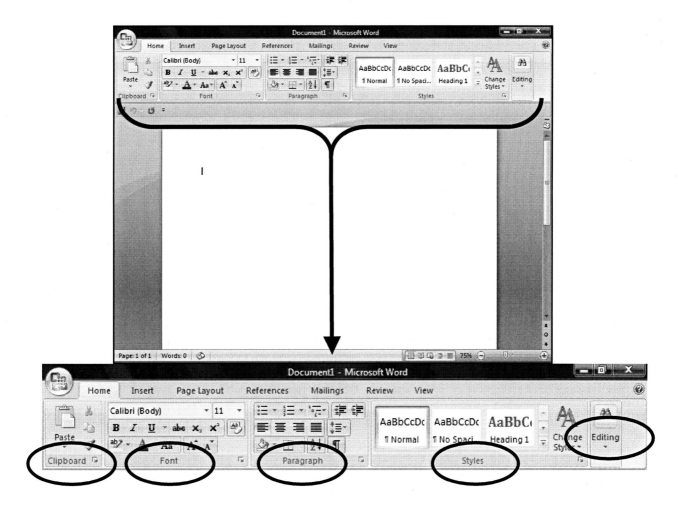

Chapter 1: Let's Get Started!

Overview of the Insert Tab

1. **Pages** – Cover Pages, Additional Blank Pages, and Page Breaks
2. **Tables** – Insert or Draw a Table
3. **Illustrations** – Pictures, Clip Art, Shapes, and Charts
4. **Header & Footer** – Insert Headers, Footers, and Page Numbers
5. **Text** –Text Boxes, Word Art, Signature Lines, Date & Time, etc.
6. **Symbols** – Insert Equations or Symbols not found on the keyboard

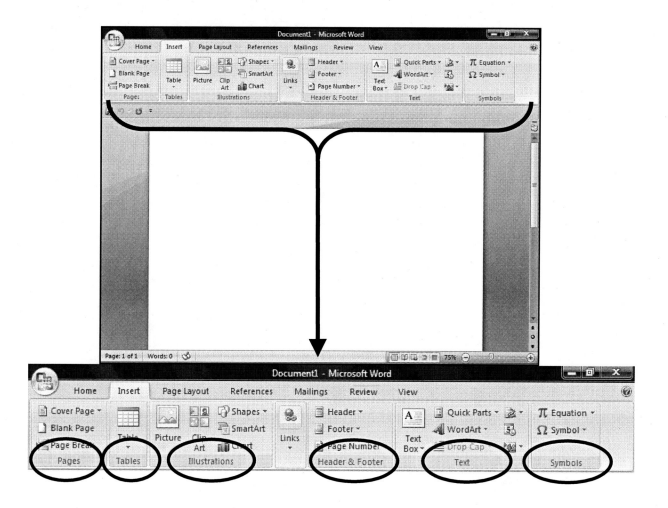

Chapter 1: Let's Get Started!

Overview of the Page Layout Tab

1. **Themes** – Change the overall design of the document including colors, fonts, and effects
2. **Page Setup** – Margins, Page Orientation, Columns, Hyphenation, etc.
3. **Page Background –** Watermarks, Background Color, and Page Borders
4. **Paragraph –** Indents and Spacing
5. **Arrange** – Position Objects, Text Wrapping, etc.

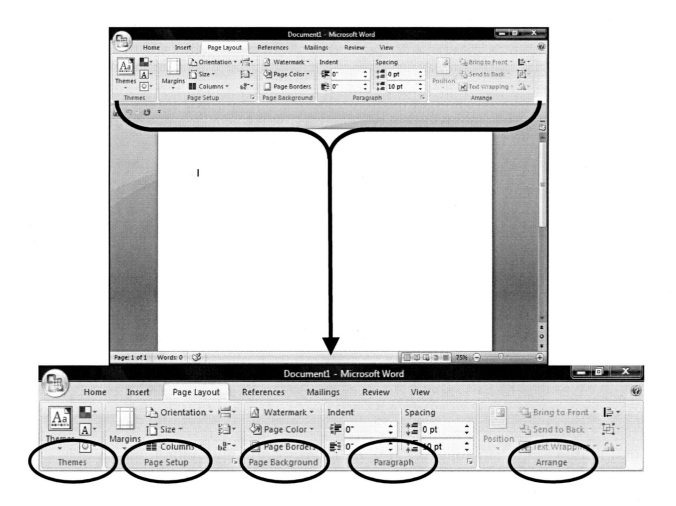

Chapter 1: Let's Get Started!

Overview of the References Tab

1. **Table of Contents** – Create/Edit a Table of Contents
2. **Footnotes** – Add/Locate Footnotes
3. **Citations & Bibliography** – Manages Citations, Style, Sources, Bibliography, etc.
4. **Captions** – Insert a caption to a picture or insert a Table of Figures to your document, etc.
5. **Index** – Add Keywords and their Corresponding Pages
6. **Table of Authorities** – Insert/Edit a Table of Authorities

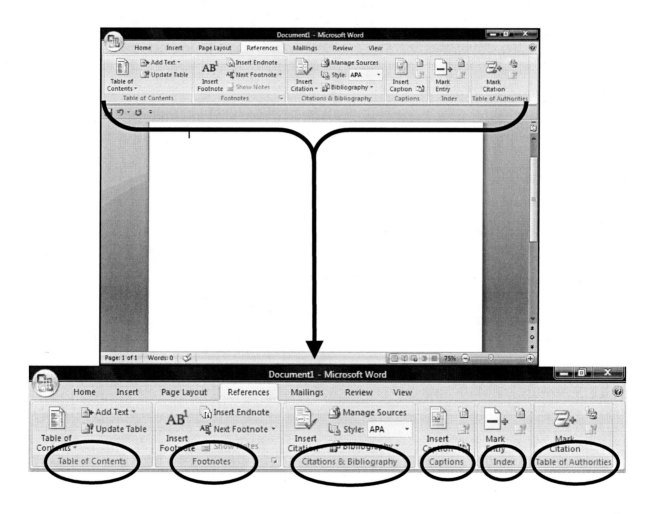

Chapter 1: Let's Get Started!

Overview of the Mailings Tab

1. **Create** – Prepare Labels and Envelopes
2. **Start Mail Merge** – Create a Form Letter and Select Recipients
3. **Write & Insert Fields –** Add addresses, Letter Greetings, Phone Numbers, Names, etc.
4. **Preview Results –** Place actual recipients into documents for Review/Editing
5. **Finish** – Complete the Mail Merge

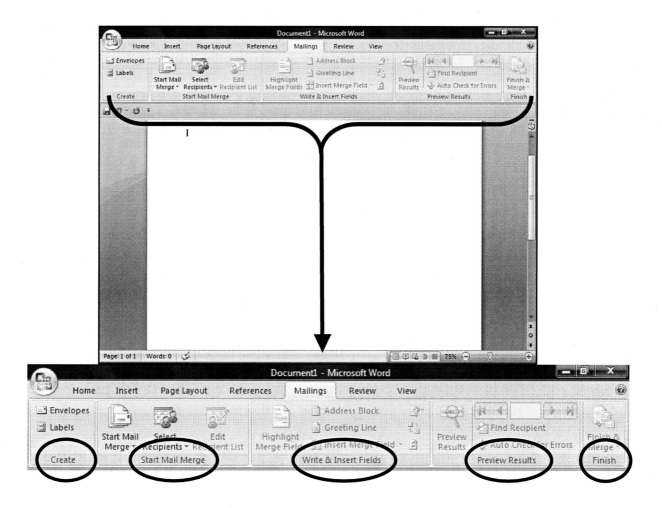

Chapter 1: Let's Get Started!

Overview of the Review Tab

1. **Proofing** – Spelling and Grammar Check, Thesaurus, Word Count, etc.
2. **Comments** – Add/Delete helpful comments to/from the document
3. **Tracking** – Track your document revisions
4. **Changes** – Accept/Reject proposed changes to your document
5. **Protect** – Stop people from making specified changes to your document

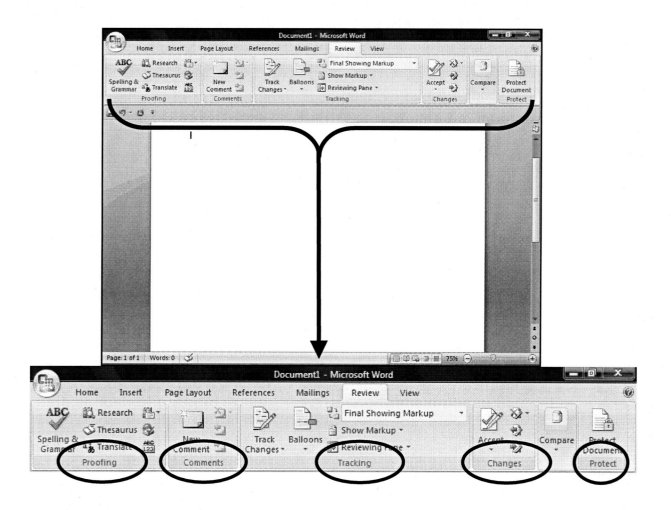

Chapter 1: Let's Get Started!

Overview of the View Tab

1. **Document Views** – Display a number of different document views, for example Draft, Outline, Web Layout, Print Layout, Full Screen
2. **Show/Hide** – Rulers, Gridlines, Thumbnails, Document Map
3. **Zoom** – View 1 or 2 pages, Magnify or Shrink Pages
4. **Windows** – Open New Window, Tile All Windows on the Screen, Split a Window into two views, etc.
5. **Macros** – Macro Options

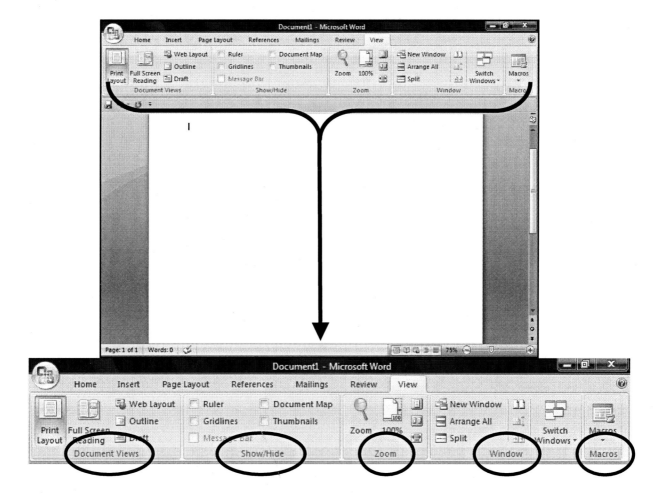

Chapter 1: Let's Get Started!

Overview of the Office Button

Clicking the left mouse button one time on the OFFICE button will display a vertical list of options instead of a group of pictures on the ribbon. The vertical list that appears is divided into two sides. The left side consists of nine "filing" options that will enable you to open new documents, close documents, save your work, and more. The right side of the Office menu consists of a list of the most recently used Microsoft Word documents.

Using the Office Button: Step by Step Instructions

1. **Place your mouse arrow on top of the OFFICE button.**
2. **Click the left mouse button one time.**
   - **A vertical list of options will be displayed.**
3. **Place your mouse arrow over the desired option.**
4. **Click your left mouse button.**

Using the Office Button: Visual Guide

Click the OFFICE button.

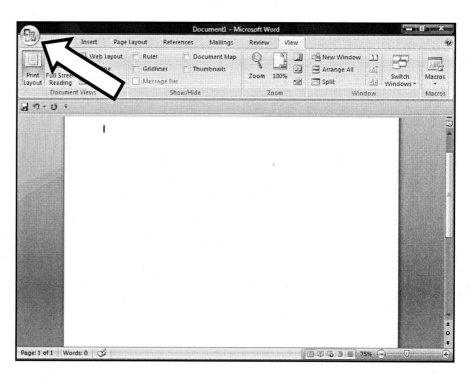

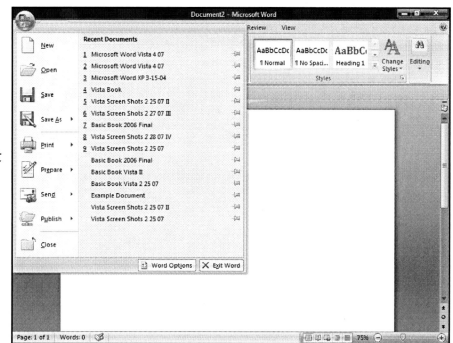

The vertical list of options will be displayed.

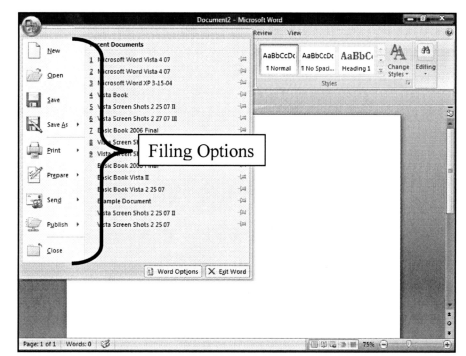

Filing options

Chapter 1: Let's Get Started!

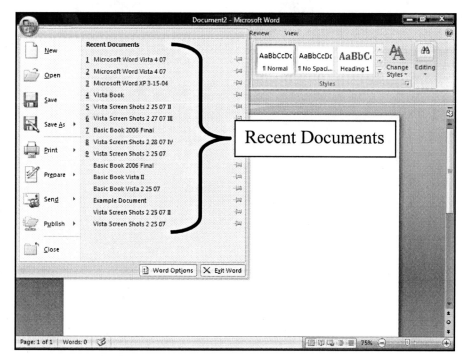

Recently Used Documents

Opening a Document from the Recent Documents List

Please note, if you are using a Microsoft Word program that has never been used before, "Recent Documents" may be blank. Once you begin using Microsoft Word, the "Recent Documents" list will begin to fill. To open and view any of the recently used Microsoft Word documents, place your mouse arrow on the "recent document" in the list (it will highlight in orange) and click the left mouse button once. A successful left click will display the selected document.

Opening a Document from the Recent Documents List: Step by Step Instructions

1. **Click the OFFICE Button.**
2. **Place your mouse arrow on the name of the document in "Recent Documents" section you want to open.**
3. **Click your left mouse button one time.**

Chapter 1: Let's Get Started!

Opening a Document from the Recent Documents List: Visual Guide

Step 1:
Click the
Office Button

Step 2:
Place the
mouse arrow
on the name of
document in
"Recent
Documents"
section you
want to open.

Step 3:
Click the left
mouse button
one time.

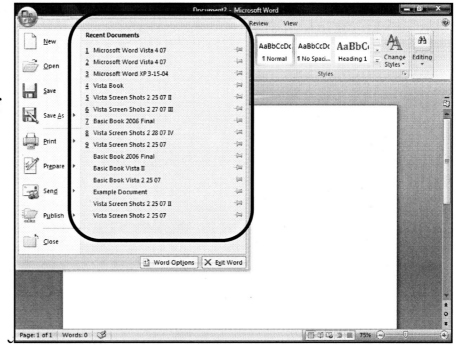

Chapter 1: Let's Get Started!

Using the "File" Options under the Office Button

The left side of the Office menu contains nine different "filing" topics. Notice that some topics such as SAVE AS and PRINT have arrows next to them that are pointing to the right. These arrows indicate there is more information under that topic heading. To see the additional topics, place your mouse arrow on the topic with the arrow.

In this example, place your mouse arrow on top of PRINT. PRINT will become highlighted in orange, and a submenu will appear displaying the various available print options. In PRINT, there are three additional options: PRINT, QUICK PRINT, and PRINT PREVIEW. To select an item in the submenu, you must slide your mouse arrow into the submenu without moving outside the orange highlight. If you move the mouse arrow outside the orange highlight, the submenu will disappear. If the submenu disappears, move your mouse arrow back onto PRINT and try again.

After you have moved your mouse arrow into the submenu, move your mouse arrow up or down within the submenu until it is directly on top of the desired option. The option will become highlighted in orange. Click the left mouse button one time to select (activate) the option. In this example, move your mouse arrow on top of the option PRINT to highlight it. Once PRINT is highlighted, click the left mouse button one time to tell the computer that you want to print your document. If you click successfully on the option PRINT, the print screen will open on your computer screen. Since we were only using the PRINT option as an example, click the close button (X) to exit the print screen and continue on to the next section.

Using the "File" Options under the Office Button: Step by Step Instructions

1. **Click the OFFICE Button.**
2. **Place your mouse arrow on the PRINT option.**
   - **The Print submenu will appear.**
3. **Slide the mouse arrow into the submenu and on top of the option PRINT.**
4. **Click your left mouse button one time.**

Chapter 1: Let's Get Started!

Using the "File" Options under the Office Button: Visual Guide

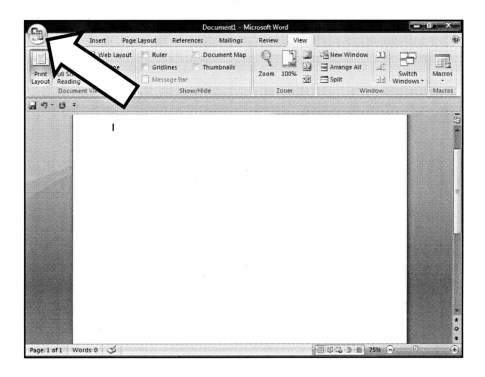

Step 1:
Click the
OFFICE
button.

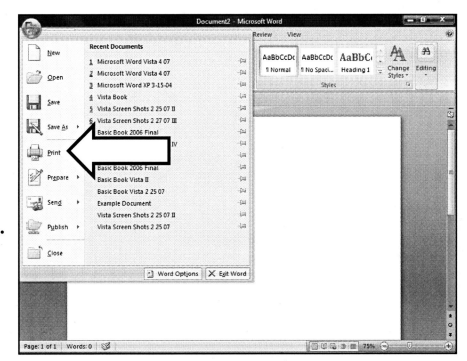

Step 2:
Place the
mouse arrow
on top of the
PRINT option.

Chapter 1: Let's Get Started!

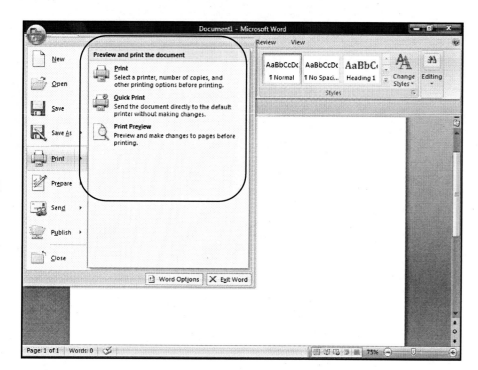

The PRINT submenu will be displayed.

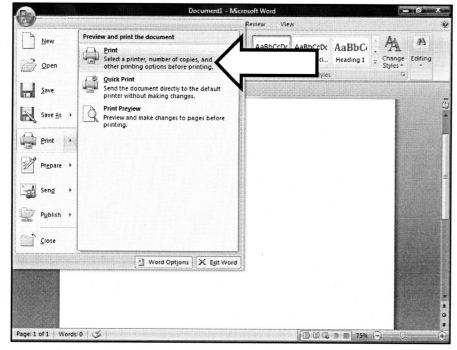

Step 3:
Slide the mouse arrow into the submenu and on top of the option PRINT.

Step 4:
Click the left mouse button one time.

Chapter 1: Let's Get Started!

The Print screen will appear.

Click on the "X" to close the screen.

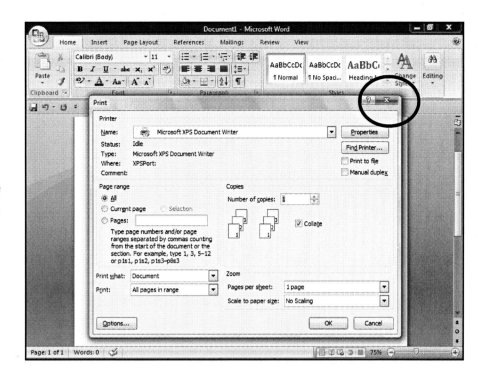

Overview of the Office Button

1. **New** – Opens a new blank document.
2. **Open** – Gives access to a previously saved document.
3. **Save** – Updates a previously saved copy of the document with the most recent changes.
4. **Save As** – Used to name the document and choose a storage location for a document.
5. **Print** – Sends the file to the printer to make a paper copy of the document.
6. **Prepare** – Prepares the document for distribution.
7. **Send** – Sends the document to other people via e-mail or Internet fax.
8. **Publish** – Distributes the document via a blog, Management Server, or Workspace.
9. **Close** – Closes the document you are currently active on your screen.

Chapter 1: Let's Get Started!

Overview of the FILE Menu.

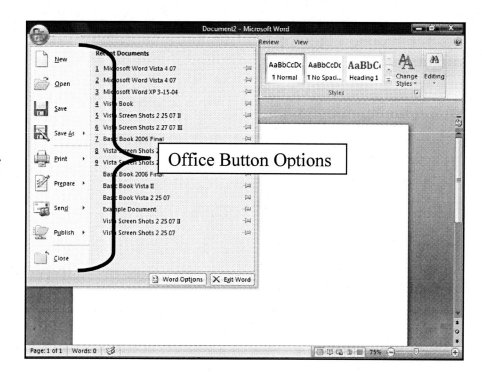

Section 4: Typing Warm-ups

The Blinking Cursor

Move your mouse arrow around the computer screen. You will notice that every time it is positioned over the blank paper, the mouse arrow changes from an arrow to a capital letter "i" (I). This symbol indicates the mouse is over an area where you can type text. Next, look in the upper left corner of the paper and you will see a blinking line. This blinking line is called the cursor. The cursor shows the exact location on the page where the letters and numbers will appear when you begin to type. Every time you hit a letter on the keyboard, the character will be inserted and the cursor will move one position to the right.

Chapter 1: Let's Get Started!

The blinking line (cursor) will always stay one step ahead of where you are typing. As a rule, before you start typing, locate the cursor to make sure it is positioned where you want to type the text.

REMINDER: The mouse symbol (I) is different from the typing cursor (blinking line). The (I) indicates that you are over an area in which you can type. The cursor shows you the exact location where your characters will be placed when you type.

Important Keys and Their Functions

The most commonly used keys include the spacebar, enter, backspace, and delete keys.

Spacebar - Located on the bottom of the main block of letters, the space bar is the longest button on the keyboard. The space bar is used to put spaces in between words.

Enter key – Found on the right hand side of the main letter block, the Enter key has a bent arrow pointing left and/or the word "Enter" displayed on it. The Enter key is used to move the cursor (blinking line) down one line. You don't have to hit the Enter key each time you reach the end of a line because the computer automatically moves the cursor to the next line. Only use the Enter key to manually start a new line. If you want to move down two lines, just hit the Enter key twice.

NOTE: When you press the Enter key, the cursor (blinking line) moves to the beginning of the next line. If your cursor is in the middle of a sentence, everything to the right of the cursor will also be moved down to the next line. Locate the cursor before hitting the Enter key to avoid this mistake.

Backspace key -- Located on the right side of the number row, the Backspace key is normally labeled "Backspace" and also has an arrow pointing to the left. The Backspace key erases one letter/space to the left of the blinking cursor.

Chapter 1: Let's Get Started!

<u>Delete key</u> - Located between the letter keys and the number pad, the Delete key usually has "DEL" or "Delete" written on it. The Delete key erases one letter/space to the right of the blinking cursor.

HINT: All the buttons on the keyboard are touch-sensitive, and if you hold a key down it will repeat the letter. For example, if you press the letter "A" and hold it down too long you, will get something like this: aaaaaaaaaaaaaaaaaaaa. Try to get in the habit of pressing a button on the keyboard and then immediately releasing it.

Type the following example letter and make any needed corrections at this time. When you are finished, you will begin to make style and formatting changes to the document.

Example Letter:

Sample Cover Letter

John Doe
Cleveland, OH 44095

Mr. Dave Jones
Vice President, Marketing
ABC Company
555 Hollow Road
Cleveland, OH 88888

Dear Mr. Jones,

I will be moving to Cleveland upon receiving my bachelor's degree in business administration from Miami University in June. A friend of mine, Jane Doe, advised me to contact you. She met you at the last meeting of the Insurance Network and said your company was expanding and in need of a marketing manager.

I know ABC Company is a leading player in regional insurance. I understand you need people who are both accurate and committed to achieving company goals.

I excelled in my coursework at Miami, and my thesis project centered on the insurance industry. I want to work for your company because of its good reputation in the community and its ability to offer excellent training and mobility. I hope to hear from you soon. You may contact me by calling (888) 888-8888.

Sincerely yours,

John Doe

Finished Letter

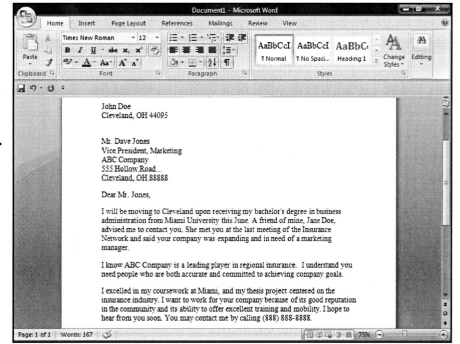

Chapter 1: Let's Get Started!

Chapter 2

Formatting Fundamentals

What You Will Learn in this Chapter
- ✓ The term highlighting
- ✓ Highlighting
- ✓ Avoiding highlighting pitfalls
- ✓ **Bolding** and *italicizing* text
- ✓ Underlining text

- ✓ Changing the size of your text.
- ✓ Changing the **style** of a *font*

Chapter 2: Formatting Fundamentals

Section 5: The Fundamentals of Highlighting

Highlighting

Once the example letter has been typed, you can explore making style changes to the text of the document. The first step in changing the style of the text is known as highlighting.

Highlighting is the process used to tell the computer what part of the text you want to change. When the text is highlighted, it may be cut, copied, bolded, italicized, and more. To highlight text, position your mouse arrow at the end of the text you want to change. Click and HOLD DOWN the left mouse button. While holding down the mouse button, move your mouse arrow to the beginning of the text you want to highlight. As the mouse moves over the text it will become highlighted (will have a blue background). After reaching the beginning of the desired text, release the mouse button. The selected text will remain highlighted until you click in the typing area again. The computer is now ready to alter the style or look of this selected text.

When you highlight text, the computer is only concerned about the data between where you begin holding down the left mouse button and the exact point at which you release the left mouse button. Think of these positions as two dots. Anything in between these dots will be highlighted. How you move from one location to another (left to right, or right to left) doesn't matter. The computer only focuses on the area between those two dots.

Now, try to highlight the first paragraph in the example letter. Position the mouse after the period at the end of the first paragraph. Click and hold down the left mouse button. Move your mouse across the text until it is positioned before the first word in the paragraph. The entire paragraph should have a blue background. Release your mouse button. Now that the text is highlighted, you can make changes to it.

Chapter 2: Formatting Fundamentals

WARNING: Don't release the left mouse button until the entire paragraph has been highlighted. Releasing the button will stop the highlighting process before you have included the entire text, and you will have to start the highlighting process over again.

NOTE: Once text has been highlighted, anything you do will affect the entire highlighted area. It is important NOT to hit a key on the keyboard because all the highlighted text will be replaced by that letter or symbol.

The only thing more important than knowing how to highlight text is knowing how to un-highlight text. If you accidentally highlight an area, simply click your mouse anywhere in the typing area, outside the highlighted text, one time. A single click will remove all the highlighting from the document.

Highlighting Your Text: Step by Step Instructions
1. **Position the mouse at the end of the desired text.**
2. **Click and hold down the left mouse button.**
3. **Move the mouse to the beginning of the desired text.**
4. **Release the mouse button.**
   - **The colored background indicates it has been highlighted.**

Chapter 2: Formatting Fundamentals

Highlighting Your Text: Visual Guide

Step 1:
Position the mouse at the end of the desired text.

Step 2:
Click and hold down the left mouse button.

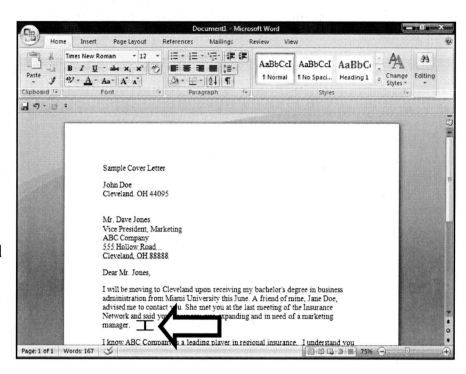

Step 3:
Move the mouse to the beginning of the desired text.

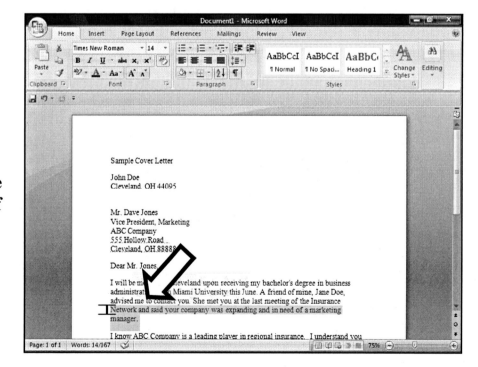

Step 3:
(continued)
Move the mouse to the beginning of the desired text.

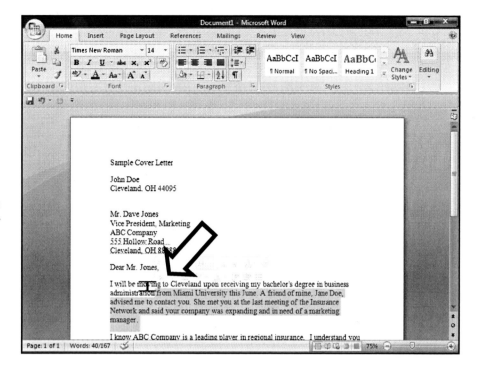

Step 4:
Release the mouse button.

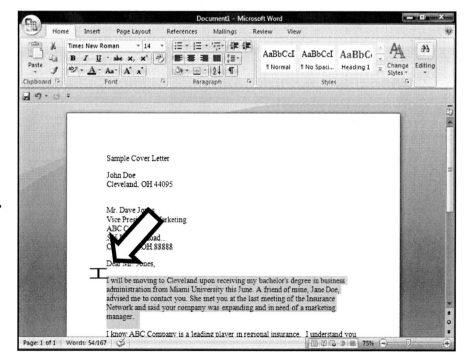

Chapter 2: Formatting Fundamentals

Un-Highlighting Your Text

To un-highlight, click the left mouse button anywhere in the typing area.

Click the left mouse button anywhere in the typing area.

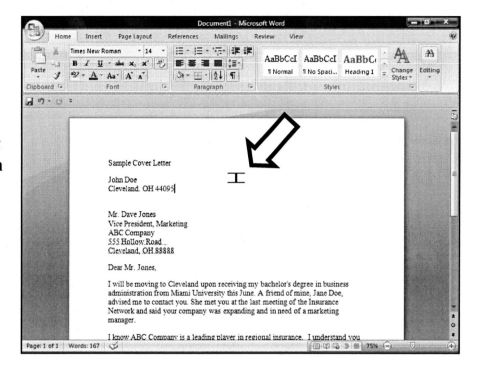

Highlighting Pitfalls

If something radically changed in your text during the highlighting process, you may have stumbled into a highlighting pitfall. If you:

- Released the mouse button before all the desired text was highlighted.
  - o Click your left mouse button anywhere on the typing screen to un-highlight the highlighted text and begin the highlighting process from scratch. Do not try to continue the highlighting. This may result in the inadvertent movement of your text.
- Hit a key on the keyboard and all of the highlighted text disappeared.
  - o Move your mouse up to the UNDO arrow in the Quick Access toolbar, and click the left mouse button. This will return the highlighted text to the screen.
- Moved a section of your highlighted text.
  - o Move your mouse up to the UNDO arrow, and click the left mouse button. The text will go back to its original location.
    - ▪ Inadvertent movement of text occurs when you release the mouse button during the highlighting process and try to continue highlighting without first un-highlighting the text and starting over.

Chapter 2: Formatting Fundamentals

The Undo Button

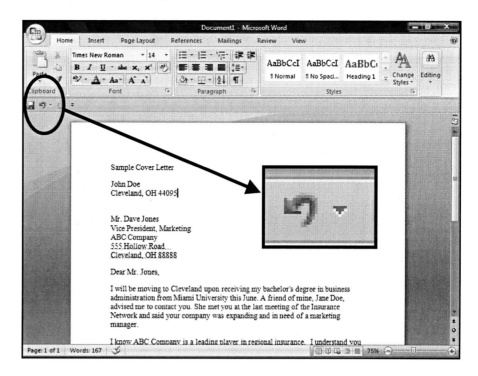

Section 6: Adding Style to Your Documents

Bolding or *Italicizing Your Text*

The first thing you will change in your letter is the title. Highlight the title "Sample Cover Letter." To accomplish this, position the mouse symbol (I) just to the right of the word "Letter." Click the left mouse button to position your cursor at the end of the text. Now highlight the text by holding down the left mouse button while you move the mouse arrow over the text until you reach the beginning of the line. When all of the text "Sample Cover Letter" has been highlighted, release the left mouse button. The text should remain highlighted with the blue background.

Chapter 2: Formatting Fundamentals

To change the highlighted text, you will use the HOME ribbon. Move the mouse up to the HOME tab, and click your left mouse button one time to display the home ribbon. Move the mouse arrow down to the FONT section of the ribbon, and look for the symbol of the capital "B." Place the mouse arrow on top of the capital "B." The "B" will become highlighted in orange. Click your left mouse button. The highlighted text will become BOLDED. Notice that the text is still highlighted. To un-highlight the text, click your left mouse button once anywhere on the page outside the highlighted area. You can now see your bolded title.

If you want to italicize your text, follow the same steps, but instead of clicking on the capital "B," click on the capital "I" in the Font section. If you want to do both (BOLD and ITALIC), you can choose both options while the text is highlighted.

NOTE: FORMAT refers to changing your text. FONT refers to the appearance of your text, e.g. size, style, color, etc.

Bolding or *Italicizing Your Text: Step by Step Instructions*
1. **Highlight the text you want to format.**
2. **Click on the HOME tab.**
3. **Move the mouse to the FONT section of the HOME ribbon.**
4. **Click the button with the capital "B" (Bold).**
5. **Click the button with the capital "I" (Italicize).**
6. **Click anywhere on the page, outside the highlighted area, to un-highlight the text.**

Chapter 2: Formatting Fundamentals

Bolding or Italicizing Your Text: Visual Guide

Step 1:
Position the mouse at the end of the desired text.

Step 1a:
Click and hold down the left mouse button.

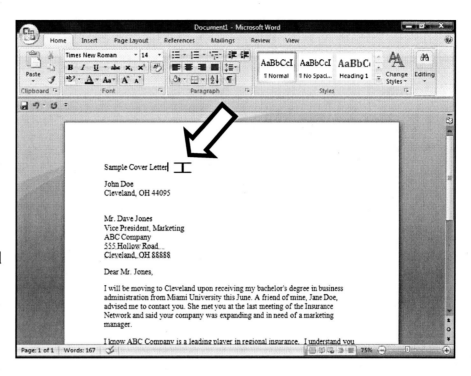

Step 1b:
Move the mouse to the beginning of the desired text.

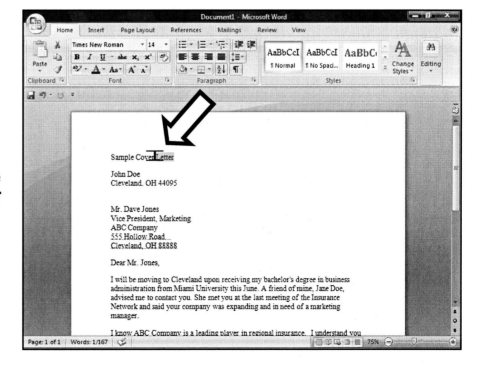

Chapter 2: Formatting Fundamentals

Step 1c:
Release the
mouse button.

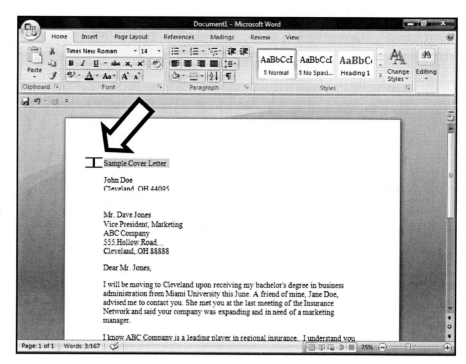

Step 2:
Click on the
HOME tab and
find the FONT
section.

Step 3:
Click the button
with the capital
"B"
(BOLD).

Step 4:
Click on the
capital "I"
(ITALICIZE).

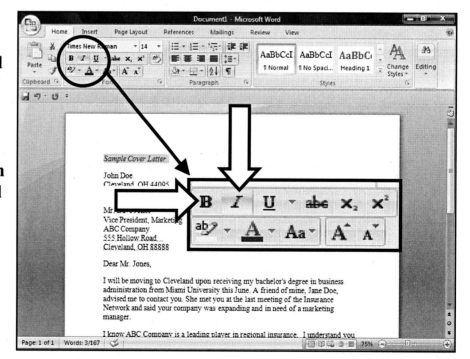

Step 5:
Click the left
mouse button
to un-highlight
the text.

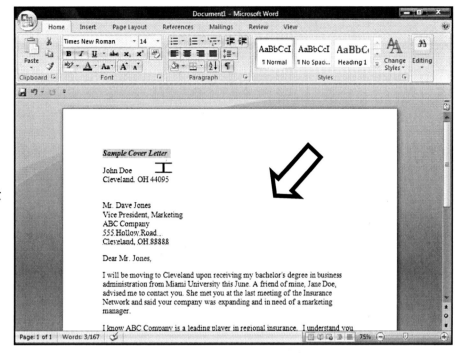

Finished Result

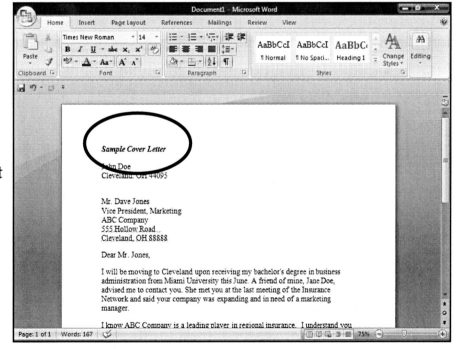

Chapter 2: Formatting Fundamentals

Underlining Your Text

The next change is to underline the title of the letter. The underline option is also located on the font section of the HOME ribbon. Before you click on the HOME tab to display your font selections, you must first tell the computer what text you want to change by highlighting the text. Highlight the title "Sample Cover Letter." To accomplish this, position the mouse symbol (I) to the right of the word "Letter." Click and hold the left mouse button down while you move the mouse over the text until you reach the beginning of the line. When the title "Sample Cover Letter" has been highlighted, release the left mouse button. The text should remain highlighted with the blue background. Now click on the HOME tab, and position the mouse over the FONT section of the HOME ribbon. Located just to the right of the capital "B" and capital "I" is an underlined capital "U." If you click the left mouse button one time on the capital "U," the highlighted text will become underlined. If you click on the capital "U" one more time while the selected text is still highlighted the underline will disappear. After underlining the highlighted text, click anywhere else on the page and the text will un-highlighted. Congratulations you have just successfully underlined your text.

Underlining Text: Step by Step Instructions

1. **Highlight the text.**
2. **Click on the HOME tab.**
   a. **Move the mouse to the FONT section of the HOME ribbon.**
3. **Click on the button with the capital "U" (Underline).**
4. **Click anywhere on the page to un-highlight the text.**

Chapter 2: Formatting Fundamentals

Underlining Text: Visual Guide

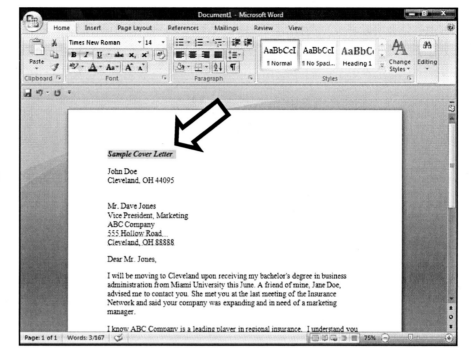

Step 1:
Highlight the text.

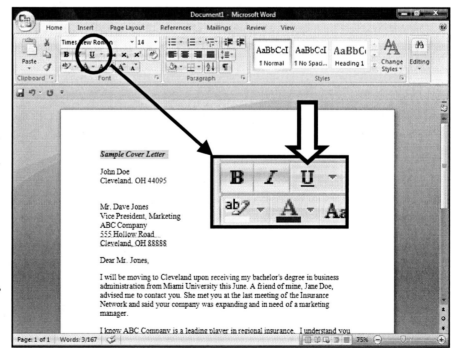

Step 2:
Click on the HOME tab and look in the FONT section.

Step 3:
Click the capital "U" (UNDERLINE).

Chapter 2: Formatting Fundamentals

The highlighted text will be underlined.

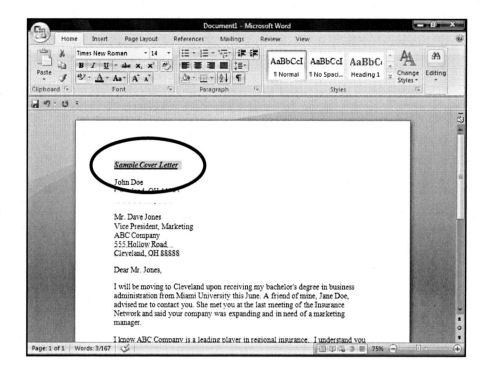

Step 4: Click anywhere on the page to un-highlight the text.

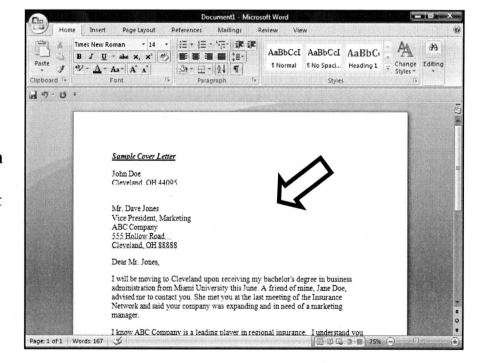

Choosing Different Styles of Underlines

Microsoft Word provides you with the capability to choose different underline styles as well as to add different colors to your underlines. To view these options, follow the same steps as just explained in the last section but instead of clicking on the capital "U," click one time on the tiny arrow located just to the right of the capital "U." A successful click on the tiny arrow will display a list different underline styles. To apply any of these styles, move the mouse arrow on top of the style you want to apply to your highlighted text, the style will highlight in orange, and click the left mouse button one time. The new underline style will be applied.

Applying Color to an Underline

In order to apply a colored underline, follow the same steps as just explained in the last section but instead of clicking on the capital "U," click one time on the tiny arrow located just to the right of the capital "U." A successful click on the tiny arrow will display a list of different underline styles. Located just below these underline styles is the option UNDERLINE COLOR. Place the mouse arrow on top of the option UNDERLINE COLOR; it becomes highlighted and a palette of different color choices will be displayed. Slide the mouse arrow on top of the color palette and click on the square displaying the color you desire. The highlighted text will be underlined in the color you chose. Once the colored underline has been applied, click anywhere on the page to un-highlight the text.

Chapter 2: Formatting Fundamentals

Choosing Different Styles of Underlines: Visual Guide

Step 1:
Highlight the text you want to underline.

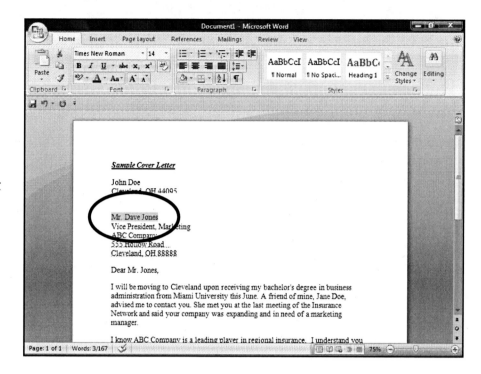

Step 2:
Click the HOME tab and find the section FONT.

Step 3:
Click the arrow next to the capital "U."

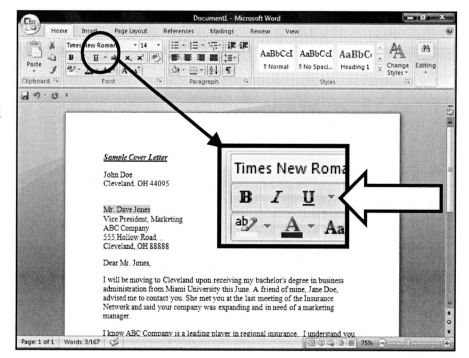

Step 4:
Click on the style of underline you want to apply.

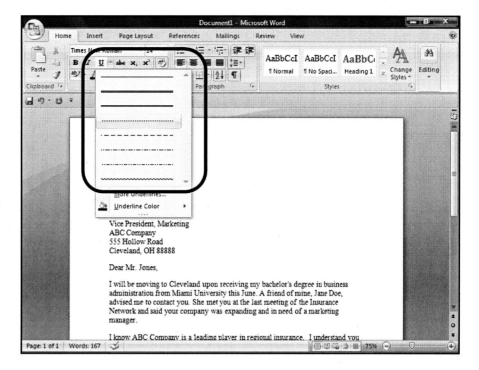

Step 5:
Click anywhere on the page to un-highlight the text.

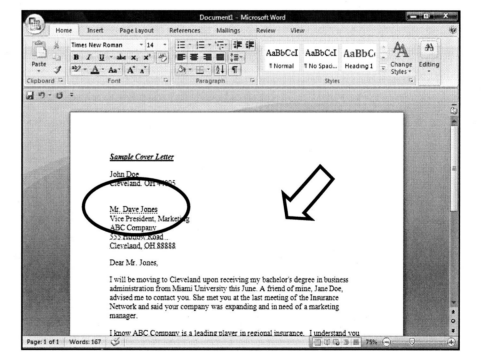

Chapter 2: Formatting Fundamentals

Applying Color to an Underline: Visual Guide

Step 1:
Highlight the text to which you want to apply a colored underline.

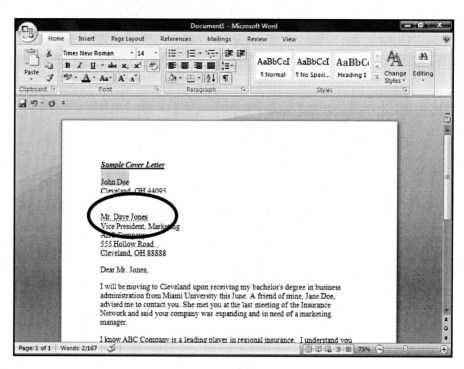

Step 2:
Click the HOME tab and find the FONT section.

Step 3:
Click the arrow next to the capital "U."

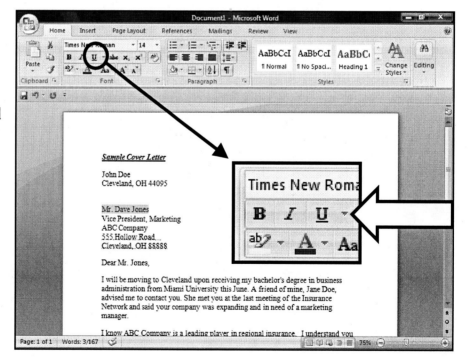

Step 4:
Place the mouse arrow on the option UNDERLINE COLOR.

Step 5:
Slide the mouse arrow into the color palette.

Step 6:
Click the square displaying the color you want.

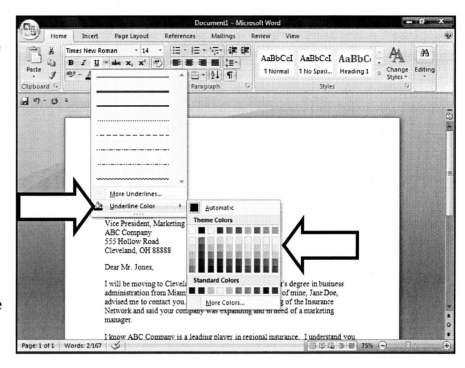

Step 7:
Click anywhere on the page to un-highlight the text.

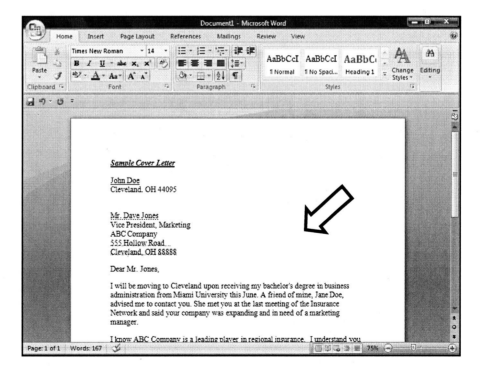

Chapter 2: Formatting Fundamentals

Changing Text (Font) Size

So far you have learned to bold and underline. In the next example, you will learn how to change the size of the text. Text size is measured in units known as points. The higher the point number, the larger the text. Microsoft Word is set up to use 12 point font. Twelve point is the equivalent of standard typewriter text. Large print books, like this one, use 14 point font, and newspapers typically use 10 point font.

EXAMPLE:

10 Point Font

12 Point Font

14 Point Font

The same basic steps used to bold and underline the text also apply to increasing the text size. In the following example, you will increase the size of the example letter's title to size 16 point font. Once again, the first step is to highlight the title of the letter. If you need help highlighting, review the information beginning in section 6. After you highlight the title, click the HOME tab. The HOME ribbon will be displayed. Move the mouse arrow on top of the FONT section of the HOME ribbon. Located in the upper right corner of the FONT section of the HOME ribbon is a number depicting the current font size of the highlighted text. Click on the arrow located to the right of the current font size. A list of new font sizes will be displayed. Click on any font size from the list, and the highlighted text will reflect the selected font size. When you have selected the desired font size, click anywhere on the page to un-highlight the text.

Changing the Size of Your Text: Step by Step Instructions

1. **Highlight the text.**
2. **Click the HOME tab.**
3. **Click the arrow located next to the Current Font Size box.**
4. **Click on your desired font size from the displayed list of font sizes.**
5. **Click anywhere on the page to un-highlight the text.**

Chapter 2: Formatting Fundamentals

Changing the Size of Your Text: Visual Guide

Step 1:
Highlight the
text.

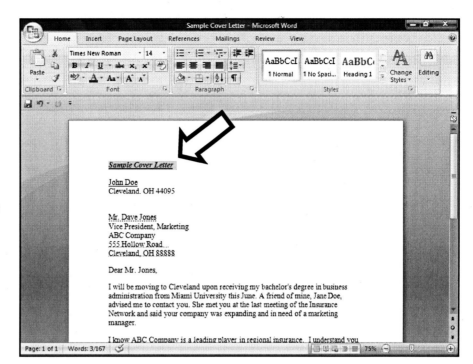

Step 2:
Click the
HOME tab.

Step 3:
Click the
arrow located
on the right the
Current Font
Size box.

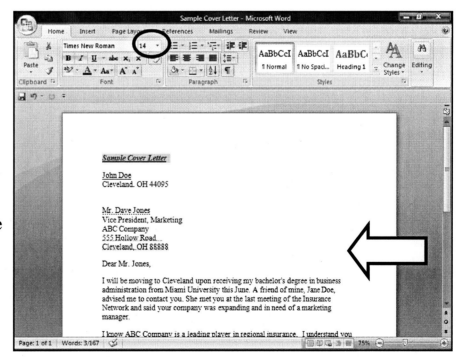

Step 4:
Click on your desired font size from the displayed list of font sizes.

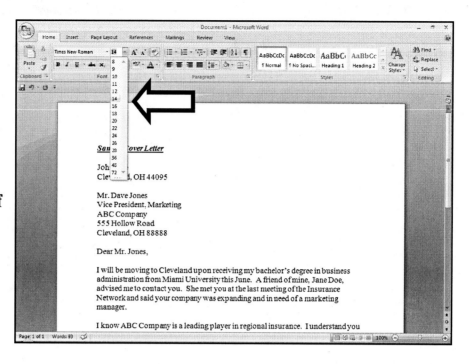

Step 5:
Click anywhere on the screen to unhighlight the text.

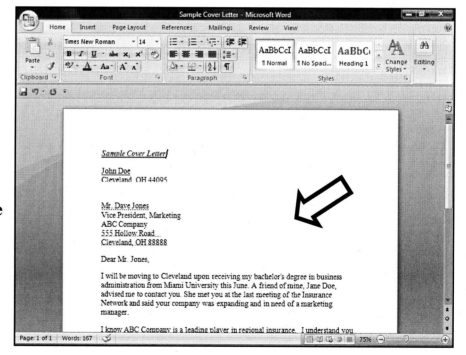

Chapter 2: Formatting Fundamentals

Changing the Text Color

You may also want to change the color of your text. The process is very similar to changing the font style and size. After you highlight the text you want to change, click the HOME tab. Located in the FONT section of the HOME ribbon is a capital "A" with a colored line underneath it. Click on the arrow located on the right side of the "A." A color palette will be displayed. Slide the mouse arrow onto the color palette, and click on the color of your choice. The highlighted text will be changed. After successfully changing the color of the text, click anywhere on the page to unhighlight the text.

Changing the Color of Your Text: Step by Step Instructions

1. **Highlight the text.**
2. **Click the HOME tab.**
3. **Click the arrow located next to the capital "A."**
4. **Slide the mouse arrow onto the color palette.**
5. **Click on the color of your choice.**
6. **Click anywhere on the page to unhighlight the text.**

Changing the Color of Your Text: Visual Guide

Step 1: Highlight the text.

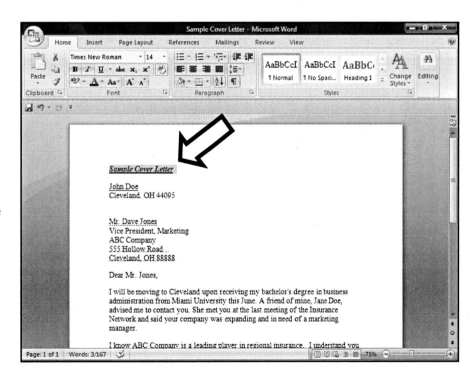

Chapter 2: Formatting Fundamentals

Step 2:
Click the HOME tab.

Step 3:
Click the arrow located on the right side of the capital "A."

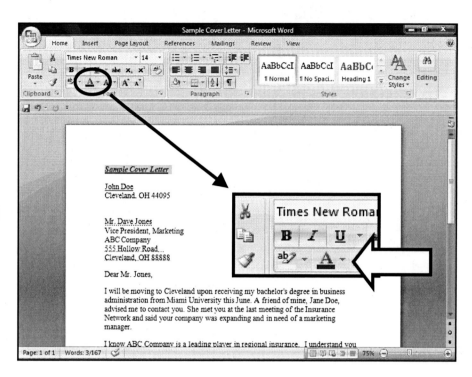

Step 4:
Slide the mouse arrow on top of the color palette.

Step 5:
Click on a color of your choice.

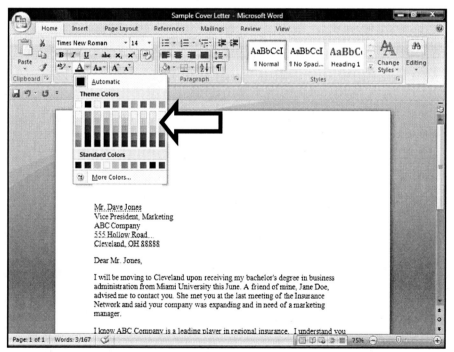

Chapter 2: Formatting Fundamentals

Step 6: Click anywhere on the screen to unhighlight the text.

(Screenshot of a Microsoft Word document titled "Sample Cover Letter - Microsoft Word" showing the Home ribbon and a cover letter)

Sample Cover Letter

John Doe
Cleveland OH 44095

Mr. Dave Jones
Vice President, Marketing
ABC Company
555 Hollow Road
Cleveland, OH 88888

Dear Mr. Jones,

I will be moving to Cleveland upon receiving my bachelor's degree in business administration from Miami University this June. A friend of mine, Jane Doe, advised me to contact you. She met you at the last meeting of the Insurance Network and said your company was expanding and in need of a marketing manager.

I know ABC Company is a leading player in regional insurance. I understand you

Page: 1 of 1   Words: 167   75%

Changing the Text Font

Font refers to the way your text is displayed on the screen and is printed on paper. You can use cursive, print, or many other styles of font. Each font has a different name and look. Microsoft Word is automatically set up to use Times New Roman because it is one of the most readable fonts. Changing the font type will give a whole new look to your text and can add pizzazz to your letter. The only way to find out what each one looks like is to try them out.

Examples: ARIAL
                          COOPER BLACK
                          LUCIDA HANDWRITING
                          TIMES NEW ROMAN

The process of changing the text font is very similar to the process you used to change the size of your text. Using the example letter, you will change the font of the letter's signature to make it look like it was handwritten. First, scroll down the page until you can see the signature. Second, highlight the name "John Doe." Third, click the HOME button. The home ribbon will be displayed. Located at the top of the FONT section of the home ribbon is a long rectangular box which displays the font currently being used. If you have not changed fonts yet, the rectangular box should display TIMES NEW ROMAN.

Chapter 2: Formatting Fundamentals

Click on the small arrow located just to the right of the rectangular font box, and a list of additional font choices will display. Look to the right of the font names and you will see a scroll bar. Use the scroll bar to move through the list. When you see a font you would like to try, click on its name with your mouse. The highlighted text will change to the selected font. The final step is to, once again, click anywhere on the page to unhighlight the text.

Changing Your Font Style: Step by Step Instructions
1. **Highlight the text.**
2. **Open the HOME tab.**
3. **Click on the arrow located on the right side of the font box.**
4. **Click the Font you would like from the list.**
5. **Click on the page to unhighlight the text.**

Changing Your Font Style: Visual Guide

Use the scroll bar to move down the page to the signature line.

Step 1: Highlight the text.

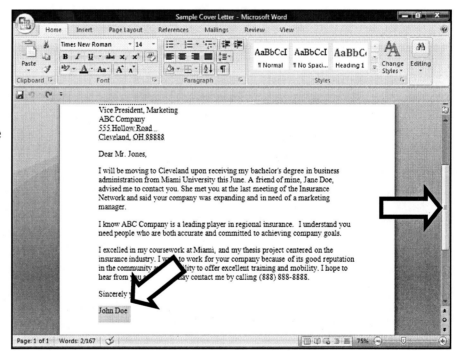

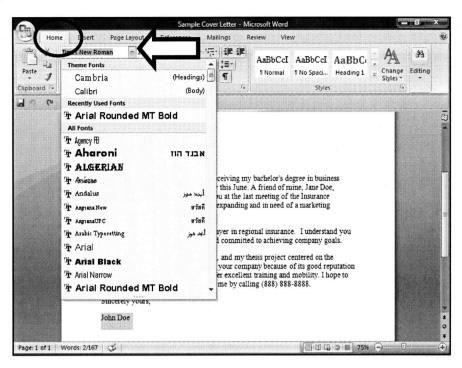

Step 2:
Click the
HOME tab.

Step 3:
Click on the
arrow located
on the right
side of the font
box.

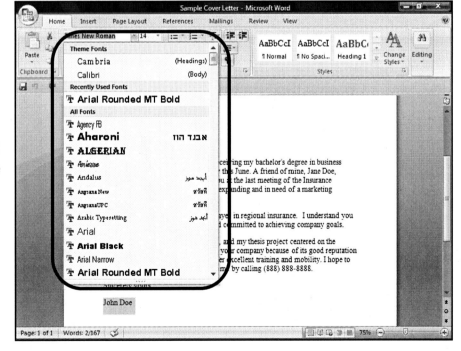

Step 4:
Click the Font
you would like
from the list.

Chapter 2: Formatting Fundamentals

Step 5:
Click the left mouse button to un-highlight the text.

Finished Result

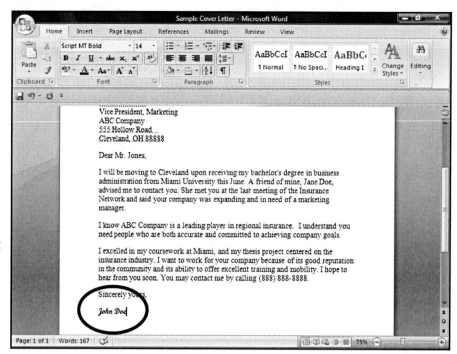

Making Additional Formatting Changes

What happens if you would like to make a formatting change, but cannot find the option in the ribbon? You can open the Format Dialog box to see additional options not shown in the ribbon. To open the Format Dialog box, click on the SHOW FORMAT DIALOG BOX button.

Once the Format Dialog box is open, click on the options you desire. Click the OK button to make your changes.

Making Additional Formatting Changes: Step by Step Instructions

1. **Highlight the text you want to change.**
2. **Click the SHOW FORMAT DIALOG BOX button.**
3. **Click the options describing the formatting changes you desire to make.**
4. **Click the OK button.**

Chapter 2: Formatting Fundamentals

Making Additional Formatting Changes: Visual Guide

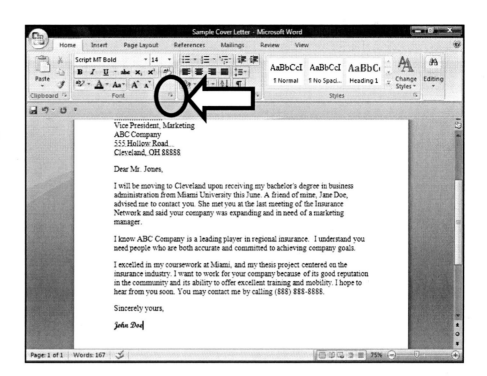

Step 1:
Highlight the text you want to change.

Step 2:
Click the SHOW FORMAT DIALOG BOX button.

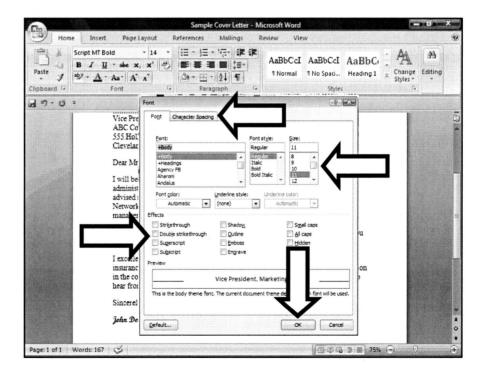

Step 3:
Click the options describing the formatting changes you desire to make.

Step 4:
Click the OK button.

Chapter 2: Formatting Fundamentals

<u>Chapter 3</u>

Saving, Opening and Closing

What You Will Learn in this Chapter
- ✓ The term "Saving"
- ✓ Saving your work to the Documents folder
- ✓ Closing a Document
- ✓ Opening a Saved file using the Office button

Section 7: Saving Your Work

What Does the Term Saving Mean?

The concept of "saving" can be best described through example. If you are typing a letter and the electricity goes out, your computer will shut down. When you turn your computer back on, the letter you were working on will be gone. You will have to start over. However, if you saved your work prior to the power outage, when you turn your computer back on, your letter will be safely stored, unchanged, in whatever location you placed it during the "saving process." For this reason it is very important to save your work frequently.

After all the hard work you put into typing the sample letter, you run the risk of losing it. The letter is currently in the computer's temporary memory. If the computer loses power, the temporary memory will be erased resulting in the loss of the letter. To avoid this potential problem, you must save the letter to the computer's main memory. Saving will enable you to return to the letter at a later time without the loss of any saved information.

The saving process is not difficult. The hard part is remembering where you saved the files and what you named them, so you can find them easily in the future. Microsoft Word is set up to store all your letters in a folder called "Documents." This folder is located on the computer's main memory referred to as the hard drive. You are going to save the example letter in the "Documents" folder.

The Saving Process

To start the save process, move the mouse arrow up to the Office button. Click the left mouse button once to open the OFFICE button. Notice there are two save options in the Office button menu. These options are SAVE and SAVE AS. The SAVE AS option is used to choose a location for the file and to give the file a name. The SAVE option is used after every update or change to the original saved file. Save As = Name and Location: Save = Update.

NOTE: The first time you try to save a file, the computer will ask you to give it a name. At this point, both SAVE AS and SAVE will open the Save As window.

Move the mouse arrow down to the SAVE AS option and click the left mouse button. This will close the Office button menu and open the save screen. There are three additional steps to complete the save process. First, you must choose where to save the file. Second, you have to give the file a name, and third, you must click the save button.

First, tell the computer where you want to save your work. Look on the left side of the "Save As" screen and find the words "Favorite Links." Located below this title is a list of the most popular places to save your work. Click on the name of the location where you want to save your work. In this example, click on the option DOCUMENTS. Whatever location you click on will display in the long white text box near the top of the SAVE AS screen. The computer will save your work to whatever location is written in this text box. Place your mouse arrow on the option DOCUMENTS from the list, and click your left mouse button once. The name will move to the aforementioned text box. You have just successfully told the computer that you want to save your work in the "Documents" folder.

NOTE: If you do not see the words "Favorite Links" on the left side of the SAVE AS screen, you need to expand the SAVE AS screen. You can expand the SAVES AS screen by clicking on the BROWSE FOLDERS option located in the lower left corner of the SAVES AS screen. A successful click will display the aforementioned "Favorite Links."

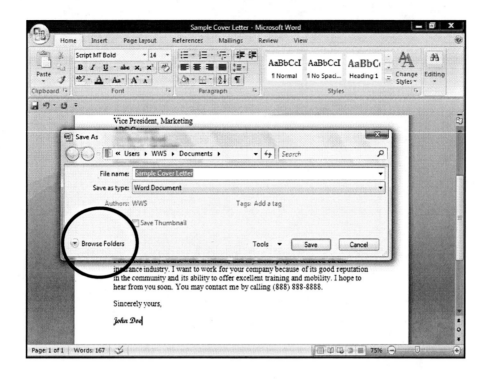

The second step is to give your new file a name. Near the bottom of the "Save As" screen are the words FILE NAME. Directly to the right of this box is a white input box where you can type the name of your new file. Giving your new file a name will help you find it later. Click in the file name box one time with the left mouse button. Any text inside the file name input box will turn blue. Press either the Delete key or the Backspace key to erase anything in the input box. Once everything has been erased from the input box, type a descriptive name for your new file into the box. In this example, the name "Sample letter" would make the most sense. Once you have chosen a location, *Documents*, and a name, *sample letter*, you are ready to click the "Save" button. The SAVE button is in the lower right corner of the "Save As" screen. Place your mouse arrow on the SAVE button, and click one time with your left mouse button. Congratulations, your grocery list has been saved!

NOTE: When choosing a name you can use up to 256 characters. The file name may include any numbers (0-9) and letters (A-Z), but not colons, semicolons, slashes, or mathematical operators (for example, the plus and minus signs). We recommended you use a maximum of three or four short words. If the name is too long, it will be truncated when displayed in lists. By keeping it short, you have a better chance of seeing the entire name displayed when searching through the computer. This will help when you are looking for your work later. If the name is too long, the computer will only show part of the name followed by three dots.

QUESTION: How do you know the letter was saved successfully?

ANSWER: If the title bar of the program window (your letter) has the name you chose for the letter, your letter was saved correctly. In this example, the title bar will have changed from "Document1" to "Sample Cover Letter."

Saving Your Work: Step by Step instructions
1. Click the OFFICE button.
2. Click the option SAVE AS.
3. Choose the location to save the file.
4. Name the file.
5. Click the SAVE button.

Saving Your Work: Visual Guide

Step 1:
Click the OFFICE button.

Step 2:
Click the option SAVE AS.

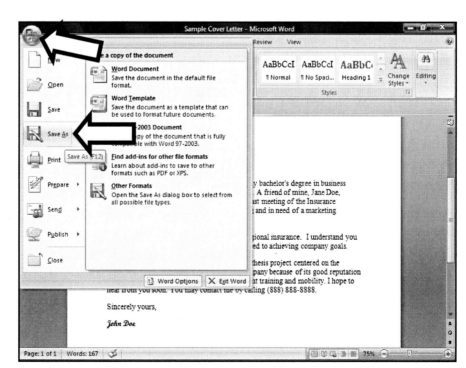

**Step 3:
Click the
DOCUMENTS
option.**

**Step 4a:
Click one time
in the FILE
NAME box
and erase its
contents**

**Step 4b:
Type the new
name for the
document**

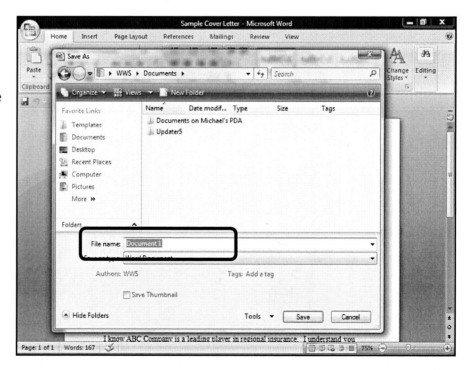

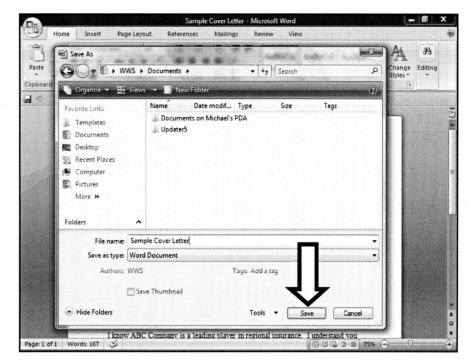

**Step 5:
Click the
SAVE button**

**Successfully
saved letter**

**. The title bar
will reflect the
new name of
the document**

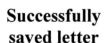

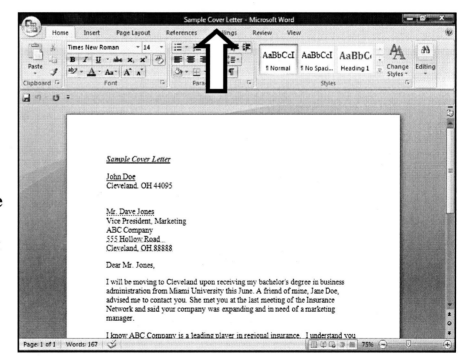

Section 8: Closing a Document

Two Ways to Close a Document

When you have finished working with a document and successfully saved it to the computer's main memory (The Documents Folder) you are ready to close the document. There are two ways to close a document. The first way to close the document is to use the OFFICE button. The CLOSE option found under the OFFICE menu will close the document, but leave the Microsoft Word program open. The second is to click the X found in the upper right corner of the program window. This will close the letter and the Microsoft Word program.

NOTE: As a safety feature, when you attempt to close a document, the computer will ask you whether or not you want to save the document. This safety prompt will only appear if you have made any changes to your document since your last save. If you want to save the changes you made, click YES. If you do not want to save the changes, click NO.

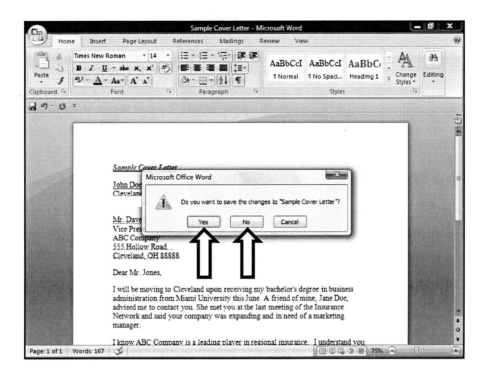

Closing a File: Step by Step Instructions

1. **Open the OFFICE menu.**
2. **Click the CLOSE option.**
   - **If a message box appears asking if you would like to save your work, you must answer the question by clicking either the YES or NO button with the mouse.**

Chapter 3: Saving, Opening and Closing

Closing a File: Visual Guide

Step 1:
Open the
OFFICE menu

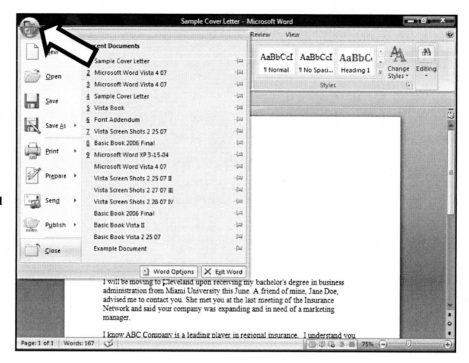

Step 2:
Click the
CLOSE option

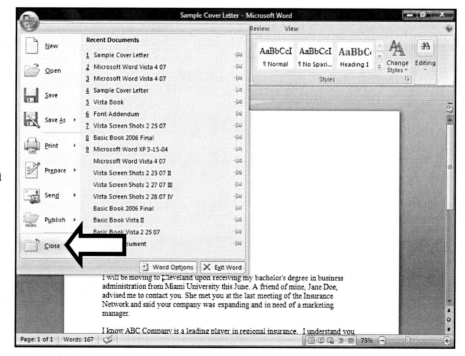

Section 9: Opening a Saved File

Opening a Saved Document Using the Office button

Now, reopen the sample letter you just closed. If you exited Microsoft Word after closing the sample letter, the first step to retrieve a file is to open Microsoft Word using the Start menu.

However, since you did not exit Word after closing the file, you can move the mouse arrow directly to the OFFICE button and click the left mouse button to open the OFFICE menu. Move your mouse arrow down the list to the option OPEN. When "Open" is highlighted, click your left mouse button. The OFFICE menu will close, and the OPEN screen will be displayed. Except for the Title bar, the open screen will look exactly like the save screen. There are two ways to access your file. The one you use depends on whether or not the name of your file is listed in the OPEN screen.

The OPEN screen always opens the folder you last saved a file to while in Microsoft Word. If you see the file name you want listed in the OPEN screen, select it by clicking it with the left mouse button. The name will turn blue, indicating you have selected it. After you have selected the file, click on the OPEN button found in the lower right corner of the OPEN screen. The document will open and be displayed for you in the Word program window. The open process is simplified if you save all your work to the same location.

If the file is not in the list shown on the OPEN screen, you will have to find the file. In this example, you saved *Example Letter* in the Documents folder. Located on the left side of the OPEN screen is the title FAVORITE LINKS. Located just below this title is a list of storage locations. Click on the DOCUMENTS link, and the contents of the DOCUMENTS folder will be displayed in the center of the OPEN screen. Since you saved your example letter to the DOCUMENTS folder, it will be displayed in the center of the OPEN screen. Click once on *Example Letter*. It will turn blue. Click the

Chapter 3: Saving, Opening and Closing

Open button located in the lower right corner of the screen, and the letter will open.

Opening a File: Step by Step Instructions
1. **Open Microsoft Word.**
2. **Click the OFFICE button.**
3. **Click the OPEN option.**
4. **Click the DOCUMENTS link.**
5. **Click the name of the file that you want to open (it will turn blue).**
6. **Click the OPEN button.**

Opening a File: Visual Guide

Step 1:
Open Microsoft Word

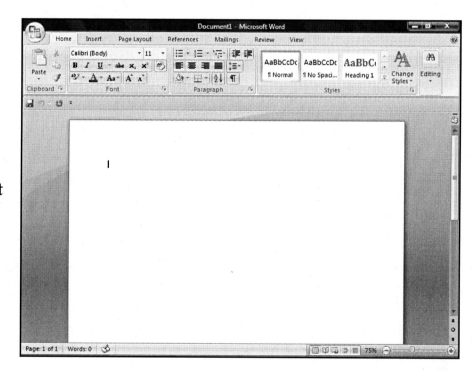

Step 2:
Click the
OFFICE
button.

Step 3:
Click the OPEN
option.

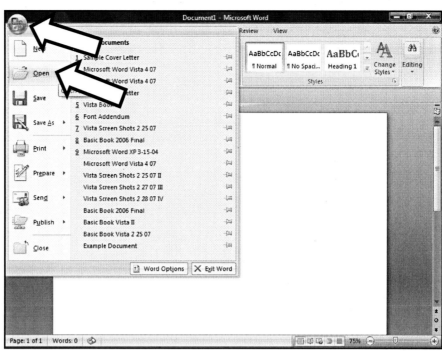

Step 4:
Click the
DOCUMENTS
link.

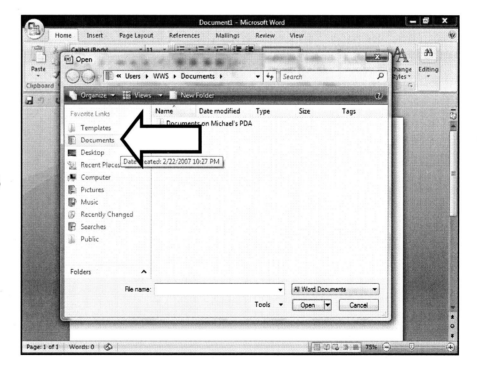

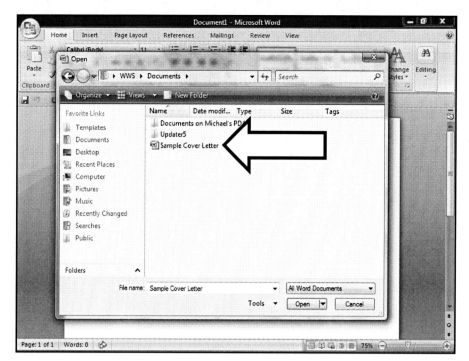

Step 5:
Click on the name of file you want to open.

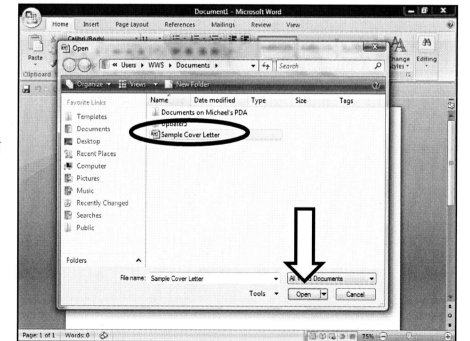

Step 6:
Click the OPEN option.

The document will open.

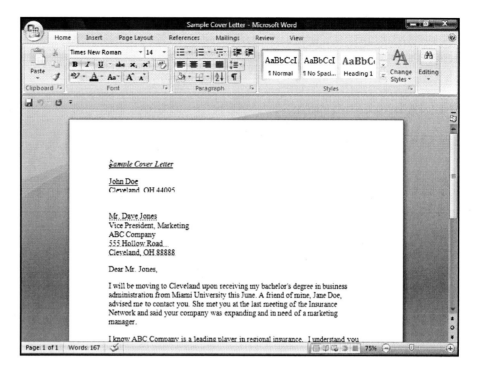

Chapter 3: Saving, Opening and Closing

Chapter 4

Aligning Your Text

What You Will Learn in this Chapter
- ✓ The terms Left, Right, Center, and Fully Justified
- ✓ Aligning text

Chapter 4: Aligning Your Text

Section 10: Understanding Text Alignment

What is Text Alignment?

The last few changes you will make to your letter will alter how various parts of the text are lined up on the screen. In this example, you will center the title and move the return address information to the right side of the screen. Before you do this, let's explore the concept of alignment.

Text alignment refers to how the text is positioned on the screen. There are four different alignment options to choose from: left, right, center, and full justification. Computers are normally set up to use standard left alignment. This means all text lines begin at the left margin. If you look to the right side of the text, you will notice that each line ends at a different point, leaving a jagged right edge. This is the result of left alignment.

Example of Left Alignment:

▬▬▬▬▬▬▬▬▬▬▬		
▬▬▬▬▬		
▬▬▬▬▬▬▬	≈≈≈≈≈≈≈≈≈≈≈≈≈	≈≈≈≈≈≈≈≈≈≈≈≈≈
	≈≈≈≈≈	≈≈≈≈≈
	≈≈≈≈≈≈≈≈≈≈≈	≈≈≈≈≈≈≈≈≈≈≈
	Centered	**Right Justified**
Left Justified		

The second alignment option is center alignment. The computer automatically centers the text on the page. Center alignment results in an equal amount of space from each side of the paper to the text. This is most commonly used for titles of documents.

Chapter 4: Aligning Your Text

Example of Centered Alignment:

Left Justified	Centered	Right Justified

Example of Centered Alignment box showing three columns labeled Left Justified, Centered, and Right Justified.

The third alignment option is right alignment. Right alignment lines up the text in a straight line at the right margin, leaving the left side of the text uneven. Right alignment is most often used in the return address section of a letter.

Example of Right Alignment:

Left Justified	Centered	Right Justified

The last alignment option is referred to as fully justified. This is the most common alignment used in newspapers. This option will line the left side of each line to the left margin AND the right side of each line to the right margin. To arrange this even alignment on both sides, extra blank spaces are added between words by the computer. Full justification is what newspapers use to make all of their columns perfectly straight on both sides.

Example of Full Justification:

Left Justified	Fully Justified	Right Justified

Chapter 4: Aligning Your Text

NOTE: Alignment is often referred to as justification. In computer terms, the words mean the same thing.

HINT: Before making alignment changes to your work, you should first finish and save your document. This will make changing your alignment much easier.

The Alignment Process

Remember to highlight only the text you want affected by the alignment change. Help with highlighting can be found in section 5. In this example, highlight the title of the letter. After you have the title "Sample Cover Letter" highlighted, click on the HOME tab. The HOME ribbon will be displayed. Located in the center of the home ribbon is the PARAGRAPH section. Located in the center of the paragraph section are four small icons (pictures) representing your alignment options.

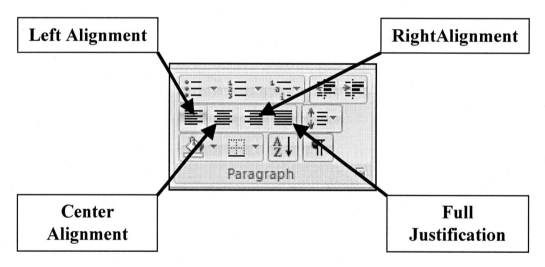

Click on the CENTER ALIGNMENT icon. The highlighted text will become aligned to the center of the page. Remember to click your left mouse button once anywhere on the screen, other than the highlighted area, to un-highlight the text. Now, repeat these steps to change the alignment of the return address section of the letter. Remember for the return address, choose Right alignment.

Chapter 4: Aligning Your Text

WARNING: If no text is highlighted when you choose a new alignment, the area around the blinking cursor will be affected.

Changing Text Alignment: Step by Step Instructions

1. Highlight the text you would like to re-align.
2. Click the HOME tab.
   a. Move the mouse over the Paragraph section of the Home ribbon.
3. Click on the alignment you desire: Left, Right, Centered, or Justified.
4. Click anywhere on the screen to un-highlight the text.

Changing Text Alignment: Visual Guide

Step 1:
Highlight the
text.

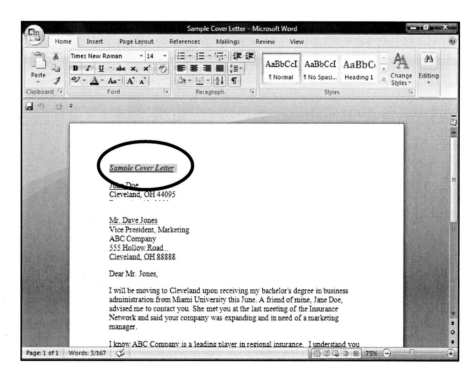

Chapter 4: Aligning Your Text

**Step 2:
Click the
HOME tab.**

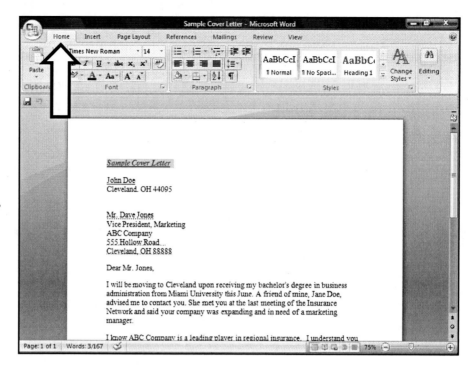

**Step 3:
Click the
CENTER
alignment icon.**

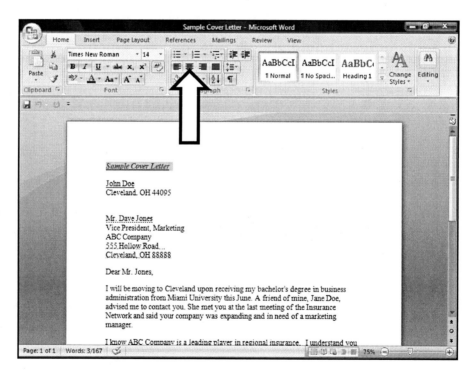

Step 4:
Click anywhere on the screen to un-highlight the text.

Sample Cover Letter - Microsoft Word

Home | Insert | Page Layout | References | Mailings | Review | View

Times New Roman | 14

Paste

Clipboard | Font | Paragraph | Styles | Editing

AaBbCcI — Normal | AaBbCcI — No Spaci... | AaBbC — Heading 1 | Change Styles

Sample Cover Letter

John Doe
Cleveland, OH 44095

Mr. Dave Jones
Vice President, Marketing
ABC Company
555 Hollow Road
Cleveland, OH 88888

Dear Mr. Jones,

I will be moving to Cleveland upon receiving my bachelor's degree in business administration from Miami University this June. A friend of mine, Jane Doe, advised me to contact you. She met you at the last meeting of the Insurance Network and said your company was expanding and in need of a marketing manager.

I know ABC Company is a leading player in regional insurance. I understand you

Page: 1 of 1 | Words: 167 | 75%

Chapter 4: Aligning Your Text

Chapter 5

Spelling and Grammar

What You Will Learn in this Chapter
- ✓ Microsoft Word's automatic spelling and grammar check features
- ✓ Making spelling and grammar changes
- ✓ The buttons Ignore, Ignore All, Change, and Change All

Section 11: The Grammar & Spellcheck Tool

Automatic Spellcheck

Two helpful features of Microsoft Word are its automatic spelling and grammar check functions. If your document contains a spelling mistake, it will be underlined with a squiggly RED line. If your document contains a grammatical error, the computer will underline the sentence or words with a squiggly GREEN line. These red and green lines are there to help you during the creation and editing stages of your work. These colored lines will not print when you print a copy of your document.

NOTE: The automatic spelling and grammar check features can be turned off and on through the WORD OPTIONS option located in the OFFICE menu.

Manual Spellcheck

After you have finished typing and making style and alignment changes to your letter, it's best to check your spelling. The computer has a built-in dictionary you can use to check the spelling in your document. Even if you are a flawless typist, it's a good idea to use spell check a part of your normal routine.

NOTE: The computer's dictionary does not include every known word. Nor does it contain all the grammar rules. The spell check and grammar check are guides and occasionally are not correct. Use your own best judgment.

Chapter 5: Spelling and Grammar

To begin the manual spell check, click on the REVIEW tab located at the top of the screen. A successful click on the REVIEW tab will display all of Microsoft Word's review options on the ribbon. Located in the left corner of the review ribbon is the PROOFING section which contains the option SPELLING & GRAMMAR. Click one time on SPELLING & GRAMMAR, and the spell check window will appear. Be aware that the spell check is designed to look over the entire document, beginning with the location of the cursor (blinking line). Spell check will work from the position of the blinking cursor, to the bottom of the document and then return to the top of the document where it will finish checking the remainder of the document.

When the computer finds a word that may be misspelled, the spelling and grammar screen will display the error. At the top of this screen is an area displaying the sentence containing the error. The misspelled word will be red. A grammatical error will be green. You have several options at this point. One option is to change the error manually. Next to the word you will see the cursor blinking. You can use the Backspace key on the keyboard to erase the error and then type in the correction. A second option is to use the computer's suggested corrections. If you want the computer to help you with the correction, look for the white box located just below the area displaying the error. This box will contain a list of suggestions to correct the misspelled word. The suggestion highlighted in blue is the computer's preferred selection. If the blue highlighted word is the correct word, move your mouse arrow to the right side of the screen and click on the CHANGE button. The error will be replaced with the highlighted word from the suggestion list. The computer will move on to the next mistake.

If the highlighted word in the suggestion box is not a good replacement, you may look though the rest of the list to find a better one. Click on the correct word to highlight it. Click the CHANGE button on the right of the screen. The error on the page will be replaced with the highlighted word from the suggestion list, and the computer will move on to the next mistake.

If you misspell a word too badly, the computer may have no suggestions. In this case you must make a choice -- you can ignore the mistake or you can try to change the word manually as previously discussed. If your change is incorrect, the computer will display it as an error again and try to provide you with a different list of suggestions. If all else fails, try to change the word to another one with a similar meaning.

Chapter 5: Spelling and Grammar

Formal names and places are often underlined as misspelled. This occurs because many formal names and places are not found in the computer's dictionary. When spell check indicates a word is spelled incorrectly, you may ignore the computer's suggestion. This is done by clicking the mouse on the IGNORE ONCE button located on the right side of the spell check screen. The IGNORE ONCE button instructs the computer to move on to the next mistake.

Often you will use the same formal names and places multiple times in a document. If the computer recognizes these words as errors, it will bring them up in the spell check screen each time the words appear in the letter. To prevent this from happening, spell check provides you with two options. The first available option is to use the IGNORE ALL button when the first "error" is detected by the spell check tool. IGNORE ALL tells the computer to skip over any future occurrences, within that particular document, of the identical word.

Just as spellcheck has the IGNORE ALL button, it also has a CHANGE ALL button. The CHANGE ALL button was developed because people tend to spell the same words incorrectly over and over again. When the computer displays a spelling error and you think you may have misspelled the same word several times, click the correct spelling from the suggestion list and then click the CHANGE ALL button. The computer will replace every occurrence of the misspelled word throughout the document.

NOTE: When spell check has finished checking the document and all errors have been corrected, a message will pop up stating the spell check has finished.

Remember, after you have used the spell check tool, it's best to go back and read your letter to make sure everything is correct. The computer is not perfect. You may find additional errors that need correcting.

Chapter 5: Spelling and Grammar

Grammar Check

The spell check tool also checks for grammatical errors. The computer provides you with suggestions to fix punctuation errors, fragmented sentences, and many other grammatical mistakes. All grammar issues will be underlined with a green squiggly line. As with spell check, you can make the changes manually or pick from the list of suggestions. Remember that your grammar rules might be different from the rules programmed into the computer. If you think you are right, simply ignore the error by clicking the IGNORE button. If you do not want the computer to check grammar, you can uncheck the "Check Grammar" box located in the lower left side of the check spelling screen. To uncheck this option, click in the "Check Grammar" box and the small check mark will disappear. To reinstate grammar check, click the "Check Grammar" box again and the check mark will reappear.

To try the spelling and grammar functions, go back into the letter and misspell some words. Replace the period at the end of any sentence with a comma. Use the following instructions to see how spell check and grammar check work.

Spelling and Grammar Check: Step by Step Instructions

1. **Click the REVIEW tab.**
2. **Click the SPELLING & GRAMMAR option.**
   - **The program will begin checking your document for spelling mistakes and grammatical errors.**
   - **Spelling errors will be highlighted in red and a list of correct spellings will be provided. Grammatical errors will be highlighted in green.**
3. **Click on the correct spelling of the word from the list provided or click on the correct grammatical choice.**
4. **Click the CHANGE button.**
   - **If you do not wish to change the spelling, you may click the IGNORE button.**

Chapter 5: Spelling and Grammar

Spelling and Grammar Check: Visual Guide

**Step 1:
Click the
REVIEW tab.**

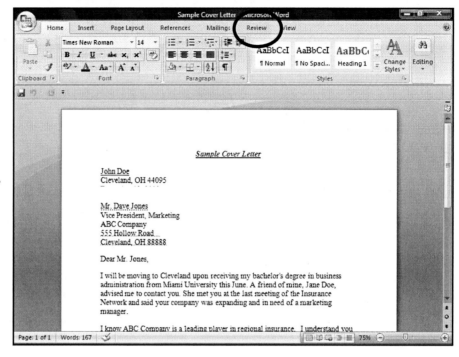

**Step 2:
Click the
SPELLING
AND
GRAMMAR
option.**

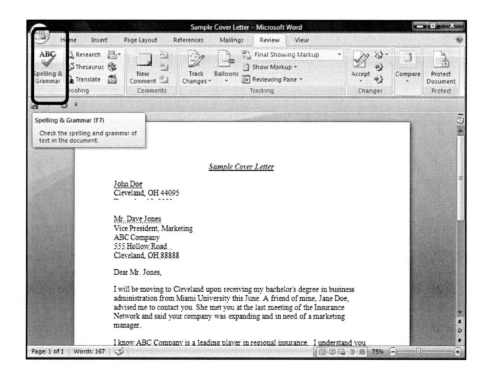

The spelling errors and suggested corrections will be displayed.

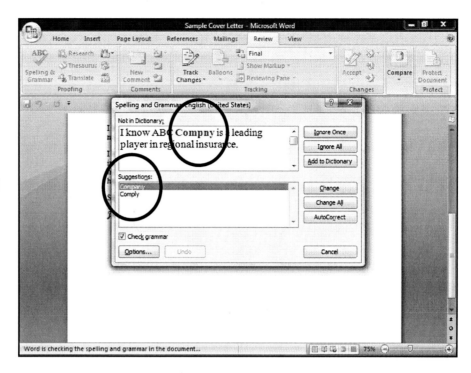

Step 3: Click on the correct suggestion.

Step 4: Click the CHANGE button.

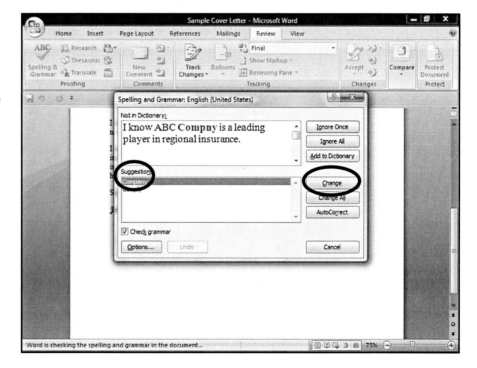

Chapter 5: Spelling and Grammar

Spelling and Grammar Check (Manual Changes): Step by Step Instructions

1. Click the REVIEW tab.
2. Click the Spelling & Grammar option.
   - The program will begin checking your document for spelling mistakes and grammatical errors.
   - Spelling errors will be highlighted in red, and a list of correct spellings will be provided.
3. Click after the word(s) that you wish to change.
4. Use the Backspace key on the keyboard to erase the incorrect word(s).
5. Type the new word(s).
6. Click the CHANGE button located on the right side of the Spell Check screen.

Spelling and Grammar Check (Manual Changes): Visual Guide

Step 3:
Place the blinking cursor after the word you wish to change.

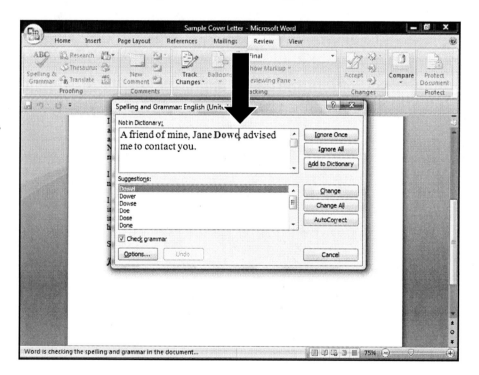

Step 4:
Use the Backspace key on the keyboard to erase the incorrect word.

Step 5:
Retype the word correctly.

Step 6:
Click the CHANGE button.

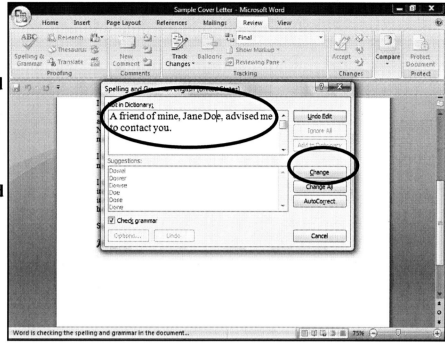

This is an example of a grammatical mistake. "Manager" is spelled correctly but there is an extra space between the word manager and the period.

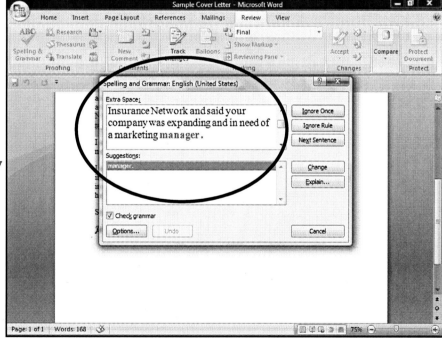

Chapter 5: Spelling and Grammar

When Spell Check has completed checking the document, this dialogue box will appear.

Click the OK button.

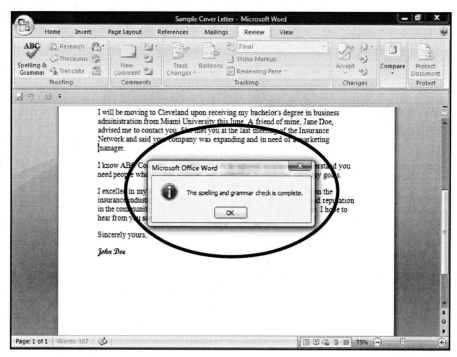

Spell check will close and you will be returned to your document.

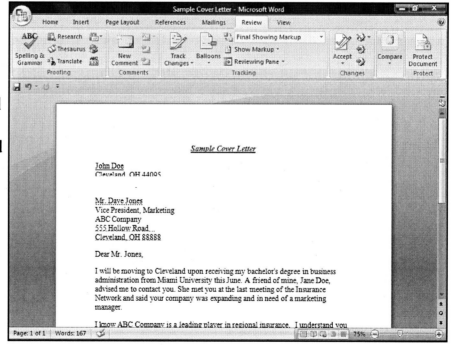

Chapter 6

Printing a Document

What You Will Learn in this Chapter
- ✓ Printing a document
- ✓ Printing only selected pages of a document
- ✓ Printing more than one copy of your document
- ✓ How to use "Collate"

Chapter 6: Printing a Document

Section 12: Printing

The Printing Process

When you have completed your document, you can print a paper copy if you have a printer connected to your computer. There is a PRINT option placed under the OFFICE button located at the upper left side of the Microsoft Word screen. Click your left mouse button on the Office button to open the menu. Slide your mouse arrow down the Office menu and click PRINT. A list of options will appear to the right of the menu. Click the PRINT option in the list. The Office menu will close and the Print screen will appear.

There are several important features on the print screen. At the top you will see the name of your printer. On the left side of the screen is the page range that will be printed. Page range refers to what pages and how many pages of your document you want to print. For example, you can choose to print every page of your document, one page, or just specific pages. The computer is set to automatically use the ALL option, meaning it will print all of the pages in your document. If you have typed a 500 page novel, the ALL option will print all 500 pages.

If you do not want to print every page of your document, you have several options. To choose a different option, click on the little white circle next to the option you want. A successful click will place a small dot in the white circle. The CURRENT PAGE option will enable you to print only the page on which the cursor (blinking line) is currently located. The print SELECTION option is ONLY available if you have highlighted a section of your text. Only the highlighted text will be printed. This option is very handy when you want to conserve ink by only printing specific sections of your text. The last option, PAGES, located below PAGE RANGE, permits you to type in specific page numbers to print. For example, if you only want to print a few selected pages which are not in consecutive order, you can type in the page number of each page separated by a comma (1,4,6,10). If you want to print a series of consecutive pages, type in the first page number followed by a dash and then the ending page number for the series, e.g. 5-8. In this example, the computer would print pages 5, 6, 7, and 8.

The right side of the print screen contains the option NUMBER OF COPIES where you may select the number of times you want the computer to print the selected pages. The computer has been programmed to print one copy. If you need more than one copy, you must change this option by clicking on the tiny UP and DOWN arrows located on the right side of the small white input box located to the right of the heading NUMBER OF COPIES. Each click of the tiny UP and DOWN arrows will change the number in the white input box.

Located just below the NUMBER OF COPIES heading is an option named COLLATE. The Collate option can be either checked (turned on) OR unchecked (turned off). The Collate option is only used if you are printing multiple copies of a document. When collate is checked, the computer will print one full copy of the document, then print the next full copy, and so on, with all pages in the proper sequence. If the Collate option is unchecked (off), the computer will print all the copies of page one, then all the copies of page two, then all the copies of page three, and so on. You will then have to put the copies in order manually. As you can see, making certain the Collate option is checked can save you a lot of time and effort.

After you choose the number of copies and the page range you want, click on the OK button located on the lower right side of the print screen. The print screen will close and your printer will make a paper copy of your document.

Chapter 6: Printing a Document

Example Print screen:

PAGE RANGE section on left.

NUMBER OF COPIES on right.

OK button on the lower right.

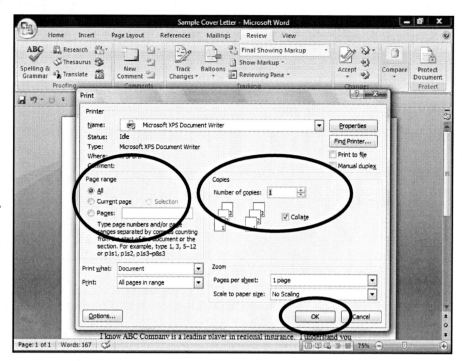

Printing a File (One Copy): Step by Step Instructions

1. Click the OFFICE button.
2. Place your mouse pointer on the Print option.
3. Slide your mouse pointer over to the sub-menu to the right and click PRINT.
4. (Optional) Select PAGE RANGE and NUMBER OF COPIES.
5. Click the OK button.

Chapter 6: Printing a Document

Printing a File (One Copy): Visual Guide

Step 1:
Click on the OFFICE button.

Step 2:
Place your mouse pointer on the Print option.

Step 3:
Click the PRINT option.

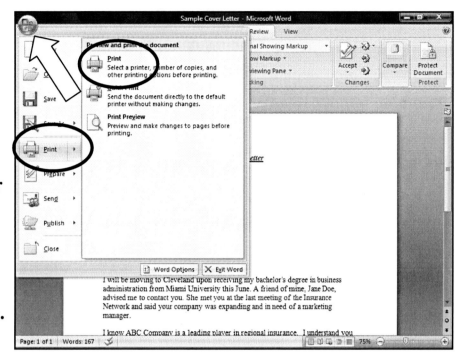

Step 4 (optional):
Select PAGE RANGE and NUMBER OF COPIES.

Step 5:
Click the OK button.

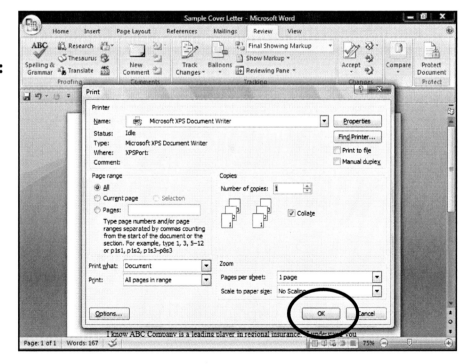

Chapter 6: Printing a Document

Printing a File (Multiple Copies): Step by Step Instructions

1. Click the OFFICE button.
2. Click the PRINT option.
3. Select NUMBER OF COPIES and (optional) PAGE RANGE.
4. Make certain the COLLATE option has a check mark next to it.
5. Click the OK button.

Printing a File (Multiple Copies): Visual Guide

Step 1:
Click the
OFFICE
button.

Step 2:
Click the
PRINT option.

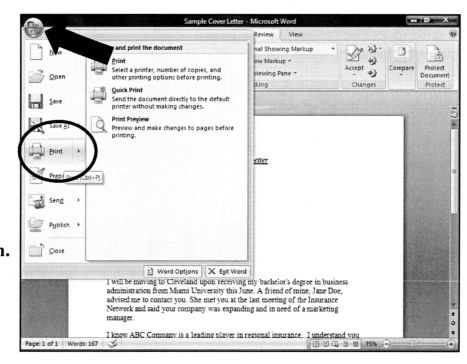

Chapter 6: Printing a Document

Step 3:
Click the tiny up and down arrows to change the number of copies.

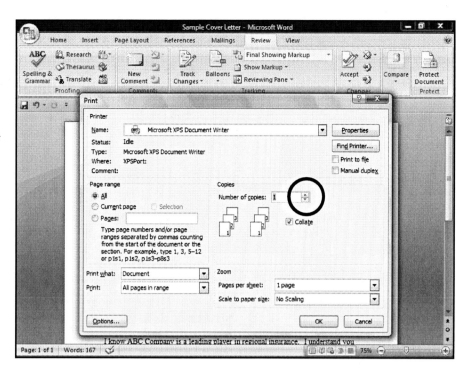

Step 4:
Make certain the COLLATE option has a check mark next to it.

Step 5:
Click the OK button.

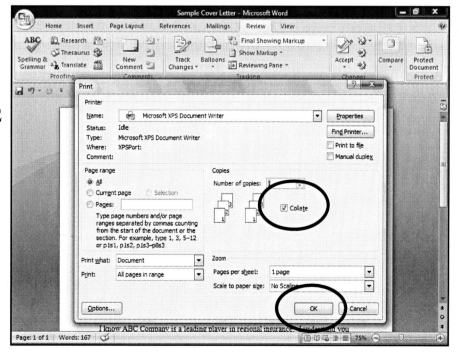

Chapter 6: Printing a Document

Section 13: Print Preview

The Print Preview Option

Another helpful feature available through Microsoft Word is the ability to see what a document will look like before it is printed. It is very common to type documents with the view zoomed in, making it easier to see the text, but also making it impossible to see what the **entire** page looks. The solution is the PRINT PREVIEW option located in the Office menu. Clicking PRINT PREVIEW will display a new screen showing you a zoomed out perspective of the document. It will enable you to see the entire page, including margins. The image displayed in this screen is exactly what will be printed out.

Located at the top of the Print Preview screen is a helpful ribbon which enables you to change how you view the previewed document. This ribbon contains options that provide you with the ability to zoom in and out, view multiple pages at once, and more. When you have finished looking at the preview screen, click on the red "X" close button located on the print preview ribbon, and you will return to your original document where you can continue typing and/or editing.

NOTE: When you are in the print preview area, you cannot make any changes to your document. You cannot type on this screen. To make any editorial changes, you must close the print preview screen and return to the document screen.

Opening Print Preview: Step by Step Instructions
1. **Click on the OFFICE button.**
2. **Slide the mouse over the PRINT option.**
3. **Slide the mouse arrow into the Print sub-menu.**
4. **Click the PRINT PREVIEW option.**

Chapter 6: Printing a Document

Opening Print Preview: Visual Guide

**Step 1:
Click the
OFFICE
button.**

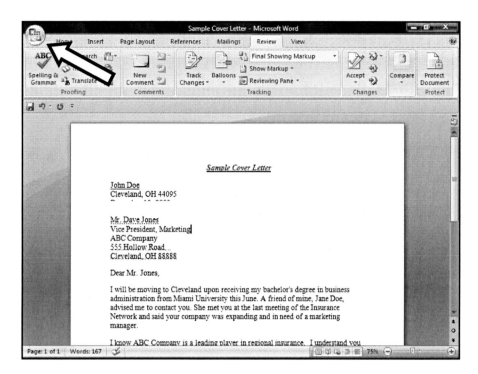

**Step 2:
Slide the mouse
onto the PRINT
option.**

**Step 3:
Slide the mouse
arrow on top of the
PRINT PREVIEW
option.**

**Step 4:
Click PRINT
PREVIEW.**

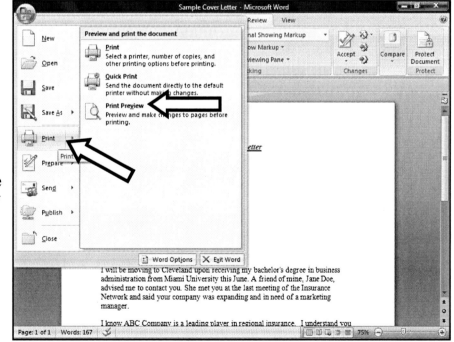

Chapter 6: Printing a Document

Example of
Print Preview
Mode

The ribbon
enables you to
change views
and print your
document.

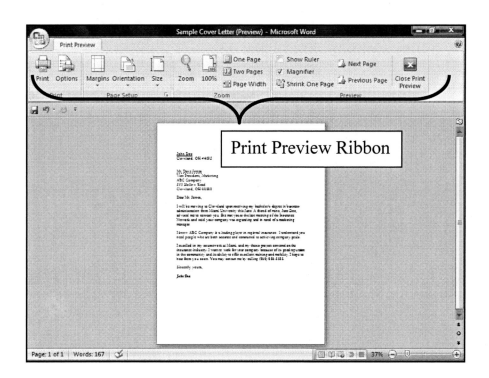

Larger view of
the Print
Preview
toolbar and its
options.

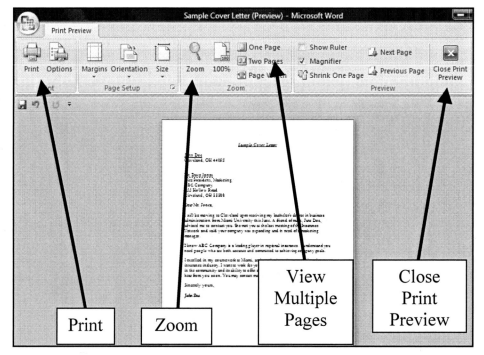

Chapter 7

Creating a New File

What You Will Learn in this Chapter
- ✓ Opening a new blank document using the Office button
- ✓ Reviewing the fundamentals of formatting

Chapter 7: Creating a New File

Section 14: The Process of Opening a New File

The Office Menu Option: NEW

If you want to start a new document, you need a blank sheet of paper (screen). The NEW option, located in the OFFICE menu, opens a new document. Clicking on this option will open a "New Document" screen. The left side of the "New Document" screen displays a list of different types of documents that you can open. In this example you only want to open a blank document. If you look in the center of the "New Document" screen, the option "Blank Document" will already be highlighted in orange. If the "Blank Document" option is not highlighted, click your left mouse button on the option BLANK DOCUMENT. Once "Blank Document" has been highlighted, click on the CREATE button located in the lower right corner of the screen. A new piece of blank paper will open. If you are currently working on another Word file, the new piece of paper will be opened in a second window. You can see this by looking at the taskbar located at the very bottom of the computer screen. You will now see two buttons for Microsoft Word, one button will correspond to your original document, and one button will correspond to your new blank document. The new blank document will be named Document1

If you open a new blank piece of paper, using the NEW option, and don't have an existing document open, Microsoft Word will place it in the program window you currently have open.

NOTE: Every time you open Microsoft Word from the Start menu, it assumes you are starting a new document and will display a blank piece of paper.

Chapter 7: Creating a New File

Creating a New File: Step by Step Instructions

1. Click the OFFICE button.
2. Click the NEW option and the "New Document" screen will be displayed.
3. Click the option CREATE.

Creating a New File: Visual Guide

Step 1:
Click the
OFFICE
button.

Step 2:
Click on the
option NEW.

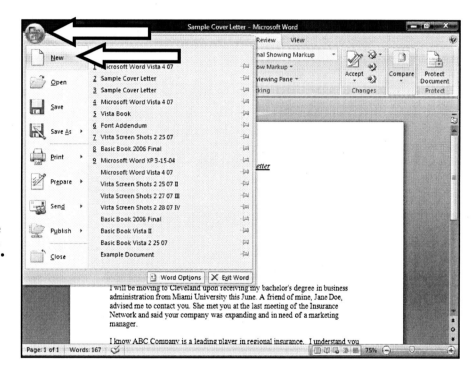

Step 3: Click the CREATE button.

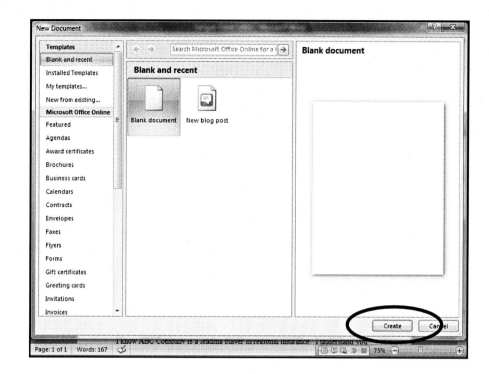

A new blank document will be displayed in its own window.

Click the buttons on the tool bar to toggle between windows.

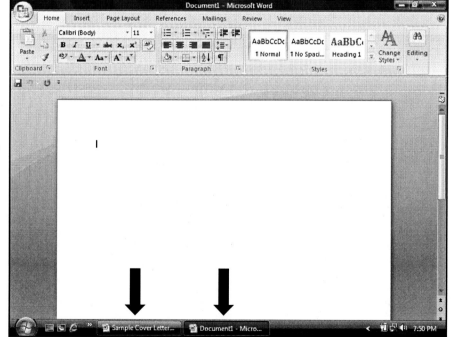

Chapter 7: Creating a New File

Section 15: Baking Cookies

Creating a New Example Document

In order to demonstrate several additional features of Microsoft Word, you need to create another sample document to use. This time, instead of an example letter, you will create a recipe which will include a list of ingredients and instructions. Type the following information into a new blank Word document.

\-------------------------------------

Chocolate Chip Cookies

Makes 2 dozen

Prep Time: 10 Minutes

Ready In: 20 Minutes

Ingredients
1 cup butter flavored shortening
3/4 cup white sugar
2 eggs
2 teaspoons vanilla extract
2 1/4 cups all-purpose flour
1 teaspoon salt

Directions
Preheat oven to 350 degrees F (175 degrees C). Grease cookie sheets. Mix ingredients and place on cookie sheets. Bake for 8 to 10 minutes in the preheated oven, until light brown. Allow cookies to cool on baking sheet for 5 minutes before removing to a wire rack to cool completely.

\-------------------------------------

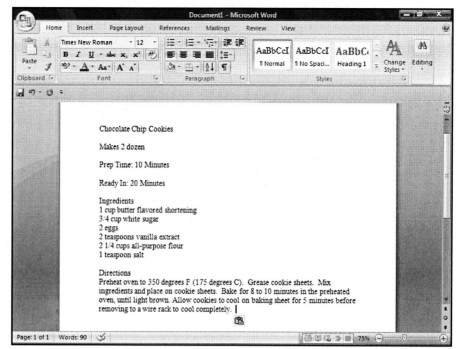

Your recipe should look like this.

Chocolate Chip Cookies

Makes 2 dozen

Prep Time: 10 Minutes

Ready In: 20 Minutes

Ingredients
1 cup butter flavored shortening
3/4 cup white sugar
2 eggs
2 teaspoons vanilla extract
2 1/4 cups all-purpose flour
1 teaspoon salt

Directions
Preheat oven to 350 degrees F (175 degrees C). Grease cookie sheets. Mix ingredients and place on cookie sheets. Bake for 8 to 10 minutes in the preheated oven, until light brown. Allow cookies to cool on baking sheet for 5 minutes before removing to a wire rack to cool completely.

Now you can begin to format (make changes to) the text.

Section 16: More Practice with the Fundamentals of Formatting

As review, make the following format changes to your recipe:

1. Change the title to Wide Latin font, and increase the font to size 18.
2. Center the title using the alignment feature.
3. Center the recipe's prep time details (located directly beneath the title).
4. Make the titles *Ingredients* and *Directions* blue, Cooper Black font, size 16, underlined, and Italic.
5. Make the remaining unchanged text bold and size 14.

Reviewing the Fundamentals of Formatting: Visual Guide

**Step 1:
Change the title
to WIDE
LATIN and
size 18.**

**Directions are
found in
Section 6.**

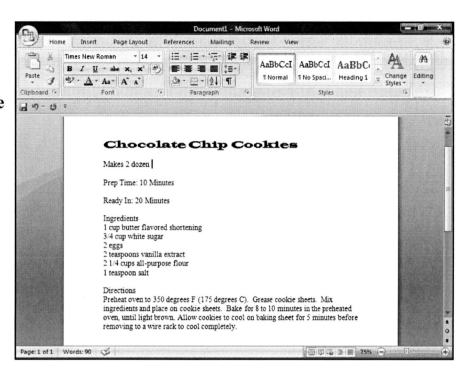

**Step 2:
Center the title.**

**Directions are
found in
Section 10.**

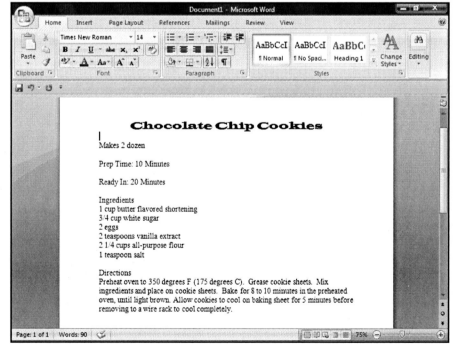

Chapter 7: Creating a New File

Step 3: Center the Prep numbers.

Directions are found in Section 10.

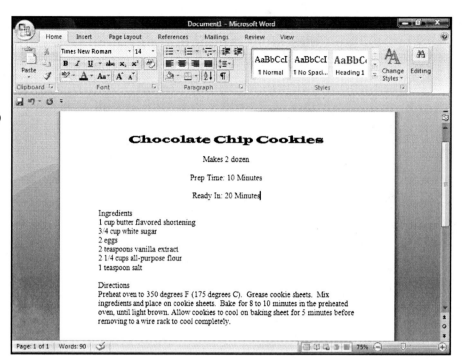

Step 4: Change the headings *Ingredients & Directions* so they are underlined, italicized, Cooper Black font, and size 16.

Directions are found in Section 6.

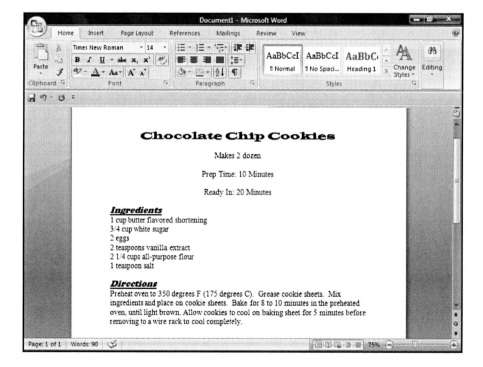

Step 5:
Bold the
remaining text.

Directions are
found in
Section 6.

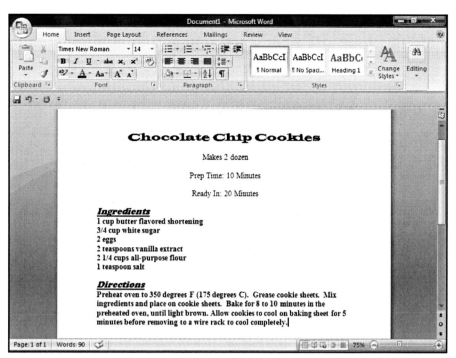

Chapter 7: Creating a New File

Chapter 8

Bullets & Numbers

What You Will Learn in this Chapter
- ✓ The definition of the word "bullet"
- ✓ Making a bulleted list
- ✓ Editing a bulleted list
- ✓ Changing the style of bullets
- ✓ Making a numbered list
- ✓ Editing a numbered list
- ✓ Customizing a numbered list

Chapter 8: Bullets & Numbers

Section 17: Using Bullets

What's a Bullet?

The bullet and number options can help you organize your work, create outlines, and develop lists. When people refer to the term bullet, they are talking about adding a small picture or symbol to the beginning of a line or a group of items. Bullets help pull lists together, improve readability and add a professional quality to documents.

Inserting Bullets

Bullets are used for lists that have no particular order or hierarchy. Before you can use bullets, you must first have a list with which to work. This is where the chocolate chip cookie recipe you typed comes in handy. In the following example, you will make the chocolate chip cookie ingredients a bulleted list. The first step is to highlight the items that make up the list. After the ingredients have been highlighted, click the HOME tab and look for the PARAGRAPH section. Located in the upper left corner of the PARAGRAPH section is a small button symbolized by three small dots (bullets). Click on this button one time, and the highlighted items will be bulleted.

If you click on the button symbolized by the three dots, you do not get to choose the style of bullet that will be inserted. If you would like to choose the style of bullet that will be inserted, after highlighting the text, click on the small arrow located on the right side of the bullets button. A successful click on this arrow will display a list of different styles of bullets. A successful click on any bullet from the list will automatically insert the chosen style of bullet. After adding your bullets, remember to click on the screen to remove the highlighting.

NOTE: When you add bullets to a list in Microsoft Word, the computer automatically indents the list to separate it from the rest of the document.

Chapter 8: Bullets & Numbers

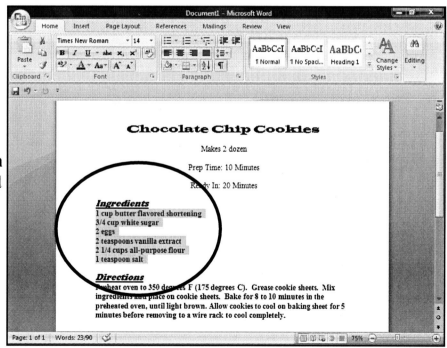

NOTE: Extra items can be added to the list after it has been bulleted. Microsoft Word will automatically add bullets to each item you add.

Bulleting a List: Step by Step Instructions
1. **Highlight the text you want to bullet.**
2. **Click the HOME tab.**
3. **Click the arrow located to the right of the BULLETS button.**
   - **A list of bullet styles will be displayed.**
4. **Click on the style of bullet you want to insert.**
5. **Click on the page to unhighlight the bulleted list.**

Bulleting a List: Visual Guide

Step 1:
Highlight the
list you to which
you want to add
bullets.

Chapter 8: Bullets & Numbers

Step 2:
Click the HOME tab.

Step 3:
Click on the arrow next to the BULLETS button.

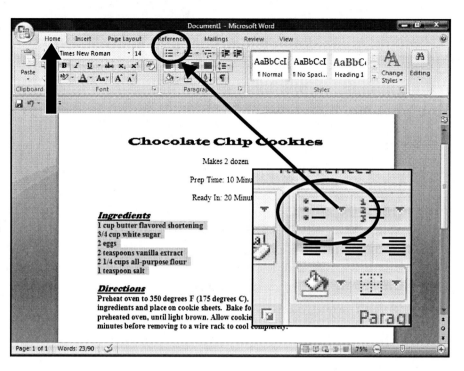

Step 4:
Click on the style of bullet you want to insert.

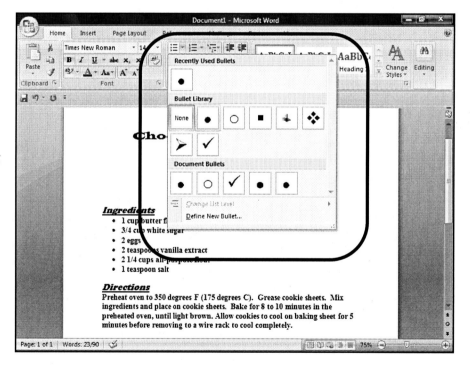

Step 5:
Click anywhere on the screen to un-highlight the bullets.

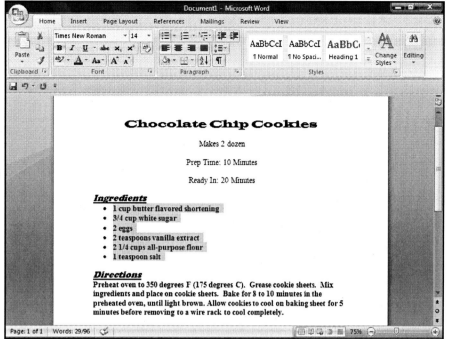

Final Product.

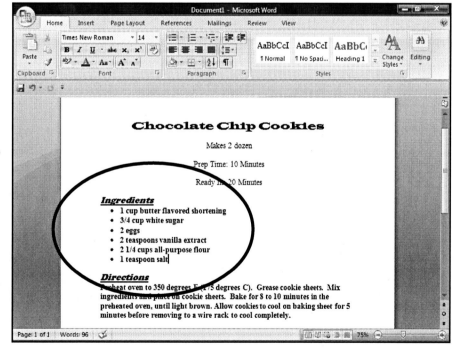

Chapter 8: Bullets & Numbers

Section 18: Adding New Items to a Bulleted List

How to Add New Items to a Bulleted List

To add a new item to a bulleted list, first decide where in the list you want to add the item. Do you want it at the top of the list, in the middle, or at the end? No matter where you want the new item to be, you follow the same process. Place your blinking cursor to the right of any item in your list, and press the Enter key on the keyboard. The Enter key will move your blinking cursor down one line, insert a blank space for the new item, and automatically create a bullet for the new line. You can then add an item to the list. Every time you hit the Enter key when the blinking cursor is on the right side of a bulleted item, it will move you down to the next line and give you a new bullet.

NOTE: To stop a bulleted list from extending further down a page, move your blinking cursor to the end of the last item in the list and hit the Enter key on your keyboard *twice*. This will move you down to the next line and cease the bulleted formatting.

Chapter 8: Bullets & Numbers

Editing Bullets (Adding Additional Bullets): Step by Step Instructions

1. Place the cursor at the end of the line preceding the line you want bulleted.
2. Press the Enter key on the keyboard.
   - Pressing the Enter key will insert a bullet directly beneath the previous bullet.
3. Type the new item.
   - Press the TAB key on the keyboard if you wish to indent the new bullet.

Practice Adding Additional Bullets

Add these items to your list of ingredients:

        3/4 cup brown sugar

        1 teaspoon baking soda

        2 cups milk chocolate chips

Practice Adding Additional Bullets: Visual Guide

Step 1:
Place the blinking cursor after the word SUGAR.

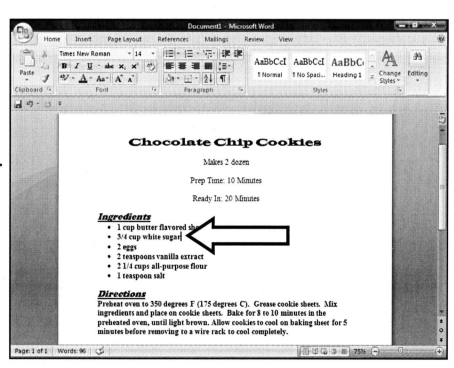

**Step 2:
Press the Enter
key on the
keyboard.**

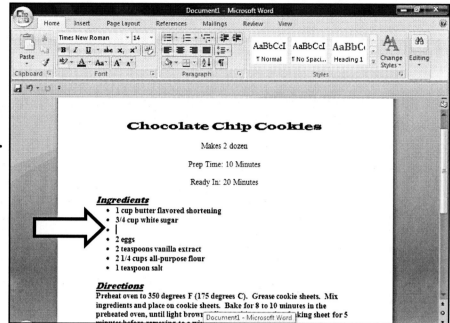

**Step 3:
Type:
¾ cup brown
sugar**

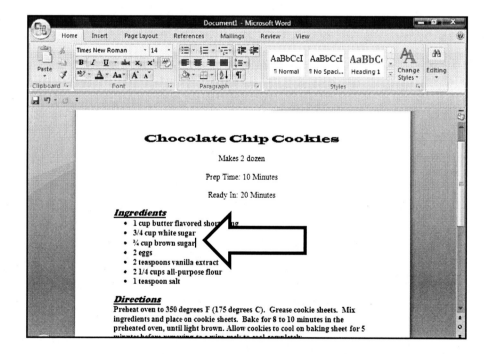

Chapter 8: Bullets & Numbers

Step 1:
Place the blinking cursor after the word EGGS.

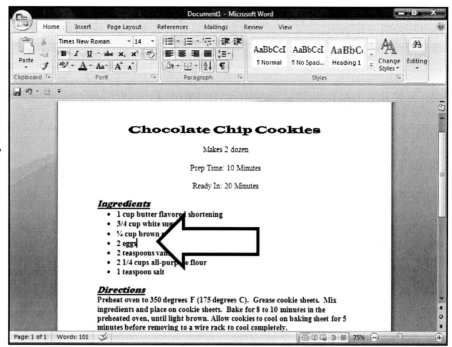

Step 2:
Press the Enter key on the keyboard.

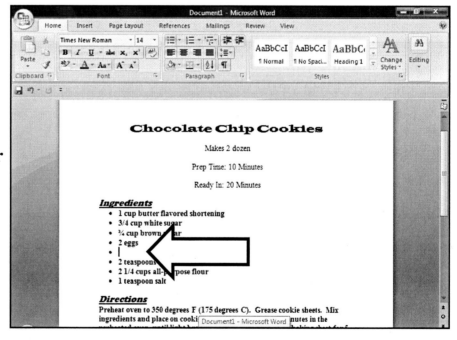

**Step 3:
Type:
1 teaspoon
baking soda**

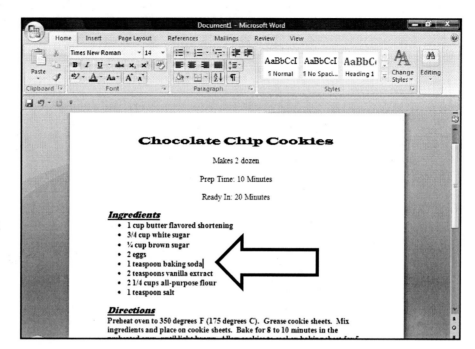

**Step 1:
Place the
blinking cursor
after the word
SALT.**

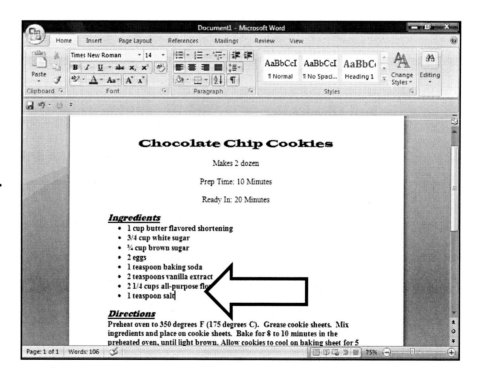

Chapter 8: Bullets & Numbers

Step 2:
Press the Enter key.

Step 3:
Type:
2 cups milk chocolate chips.

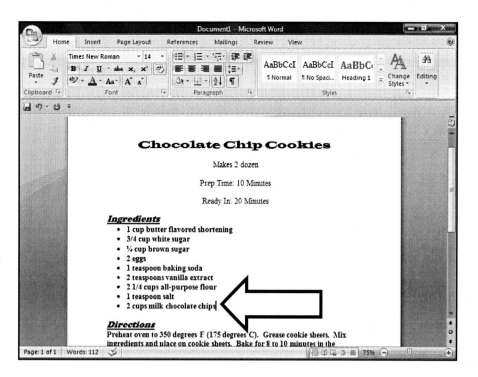

Stopping the Bullets.

The blinking cursor should be after the word CHIPS.

Press the Enter key twice.

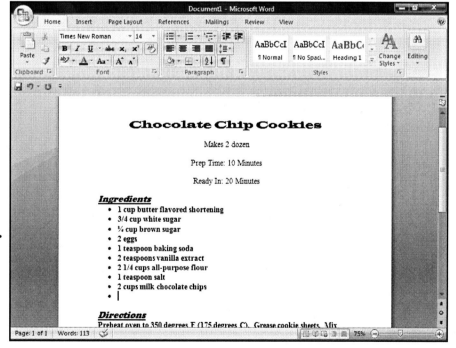

Chapter 8: Bullets & Numbers

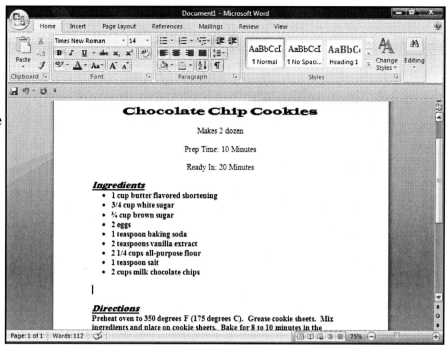

The bullets have been stopped. You can now type without new bullets appearing.

Section 19: Changing the Style of Bullets

How to Change the Style of Bullets

Do not worry if you create a bulleted list and afterwards decide you want to change the style of bullet. Microsoft Word makes the process of changing bullet styles easy. First, highlight the entire list. Next, click the HOME tab, and then move the mouse arrow to the Paragraph section of the Home ribbon. Click on the arrow located on the right side of the bullets button. A list of bullet styles will be displayed. Click on the new style of bullet you want to apply, and then click anywhere on the page to unhighlight your text.

Chapter 8: Bullets & Numbers

Changing the Style of Bullets: Step by Step Instructions

1. Highlight the text you want to change.
2. Click the HOME tab.
3. Click on the BULLET button's arrow.
4. Click on the style of bullet you want to use.
5. Click on the page to unhighlight the text.

Changing the Style of Bullets: Visual Guide

Step 1:
Highlight the
bulleted list.

Step 2:
Click the
HOME tab.

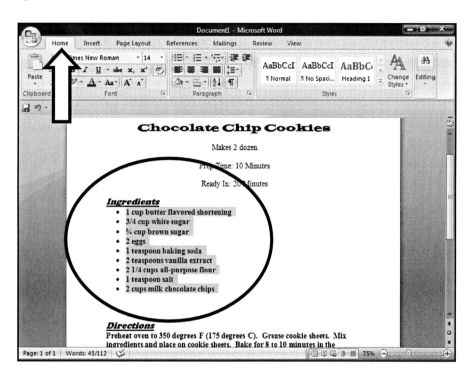

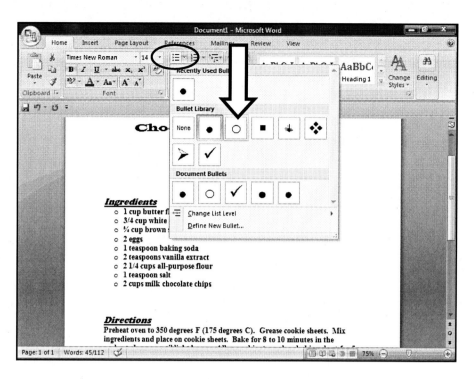

Step 3:
Click on the BULLET button's arrow.

Step 4:
Click on the style of bullet you want to insert.

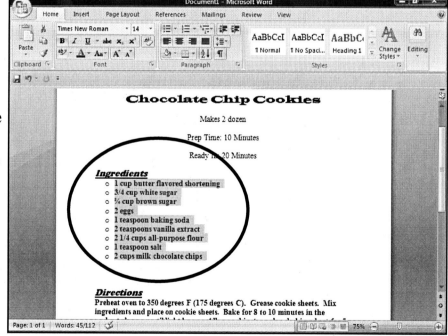

Step 5:
Click anywhere on the page to unhighlight the text.

Chapter 8: Bullets & Numbers

Final result.

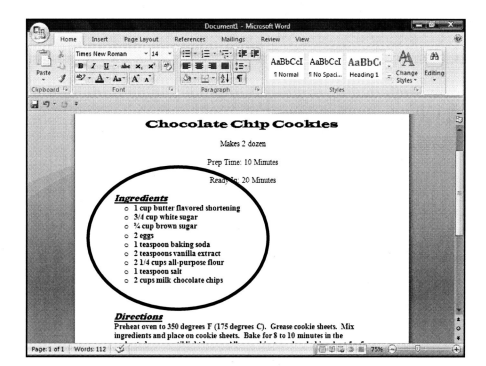

Section 20: Using Numbers

Introduction to Numbers

Numbers are used to organize lists that have a hierarchy or order to them.
Numbered lists usually begin with the number one and increase one whole
number with each new item, e.g. if you begin with the number 1, Microsoft
Word will automatically place a number 2 before the next item, etc. If an item
takes up two lines, the computer skips the second line and continues the
numbering with the following item. When new items are added to a numbered
list, the computer automatically updates the numbering to correspond with the
added items. This also works in reverse. When an item is removed from a
numbered list, the computer readjusts the numbering accordingly. Microsoft
Word will always try to keep your numbers in sequential order.

Chapter 8: Bullets & Numbers

How to Make a Numbered List

The procedure for creating a numbered list is almost identical to bulleting a list. There is only one step that differs. After you select the Home tab, you need to click on the NUMBER button's arrow instead of the bullet button's arrow. The numbers button has a "1,2,3" symbol on it. The number button's arrow is located on the right side of the button.

NOTE: If you click directly on the number button instead of its arrow, the computer will apply numbering to your highlighted text without offering you the opportunity to choose a style of number.

Making a Numbered List: Step by Step Instructions

1. Highlight the text you want to number.
2. Click the HOME tab.
3. Click on the NUMBER button's arrow.
   - A screen displaying the available number styles will appear.
4. Click on the style of number you want to use.
5. Click on the page to unhighlight the text.

Chapter 8: Bullets & Numbers

Making a Numbered List: Visual Guide

Step 1:
Highlight the text you want to number.

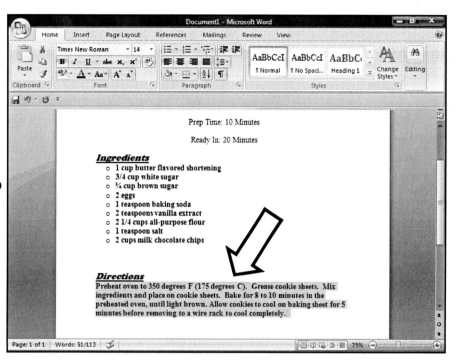

Step 2:
Click the HOME tab.

Step 3:
Click on the arrow located on the right side of the number button.

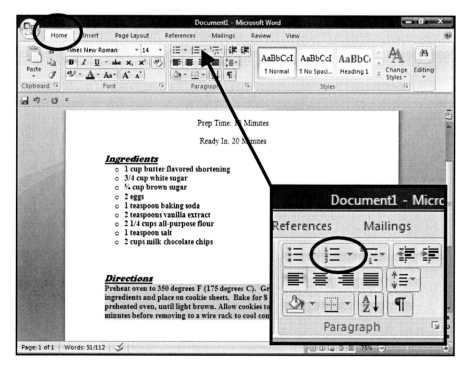

The Numbers
screen appears.

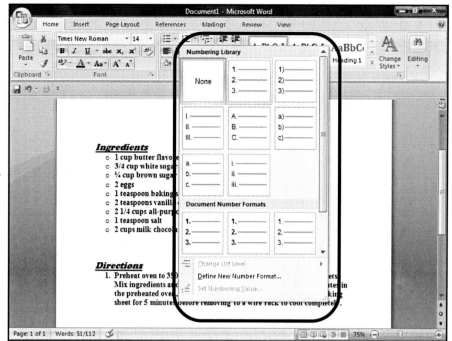

Step 4:
Click on the
style of number
you want to
apply.

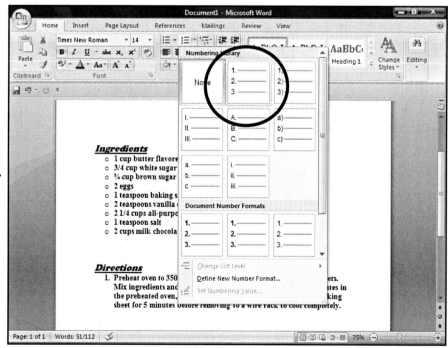

**Step 5:
Click anywhere
on the screen to
un-highlight the
list.**

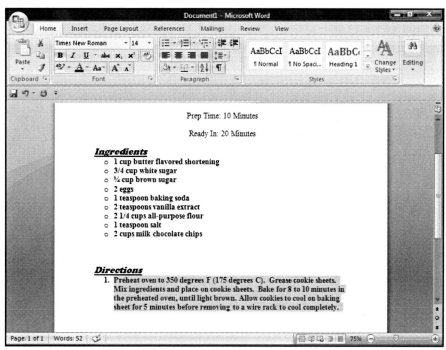

Section 21: Customizing your Numbered Lists

Advanced Numbering Options

Microsoft Word also provides users with advanced options allowing you to customize numbered lists. The customizing option is useful when you need to change the numbers Microsoft Word assigned to the items in your list, or change the number you want the list to begin with, or even control how far the computer indents your numbered list. You can access these advanced numbering functions from the Numbering options screen.

To use advanced numbering options, first highlight the numbered list you want to customize. Then click the Home tab. Click on the NUMBER button's arrow to display the "Numbering" screen. Located at the bottom of the Numbering screen are three options: Change List Level, Define New Number Format, and Set Numbering Value.

The "Change List Level" option lets you increase or decrease the indent of your numbered list. The "Define New Number Format" option lets you change the style of numbering you applied. The "Set Numbering Value" option gives you the ability to change a number from a 1 to a 2, or a 3 to a 4, etc.

To change the indent of your numbered list, slide the mouse arrow on top of the option "Change List Level." A list of different indent choices will be displayed. Slide the mouse arrow into the list of indent options. Once the mouse arrow is on the indent list, slide the mouse arrow up and down the list until the mouse arrow is located on top of the indent level you want to apply. Click the left mouse button one time, and the indent will be applied.

To change the style of the highlighted numbered list, slide the mouse arrow on top of the option "Define New Number Format," and click the left mouse button one time. A "Define New Number Format" screen will appear displaying several options. Located at the top of the screen is a drop down box labeled "Number Style." Located on the right side of the drop down box is a small arrow pointing down. Click one time on the small arrow, and a list of different number styles will *drop down*. Place the mouse arrow on top of the style you would like to apply, and click the left mouse button one time. The drop down list will close. To apply your new number style, click the OK button one time. The "Define New Number Format" screen will disappear, and you will be returned to your document with the selected changes applied.

To change a number, for example from 1 to 2, click on the "Set Numbering Value" option. A "Set Numbering Value" screen will be displayed. Located at the bottom of this screen is a white box labeled "Set Value To." Located on the right side of this box are tiny up and down arrows. Click on the up arrow to increase the value, or on down arrow to decrease the value, of the highlighted number. When the desired number is displayed, click the OK button. The new number value will be applied.

Customizing Numbered Lists: Step by Step Instructions
1. **Highlight the text you want to customize.**
2. **Click the Home tab.**
3. **Click on the NUMBER button's arrow.**
4. **Click on one of the advanced options.**
5. **Click on the screen to unhighlight the text.**

Chapter 8: Bullets & Numbers

Customizing Numbered Lists: Visual Guide

Step 1:
Highlight the
text you want to
customize.

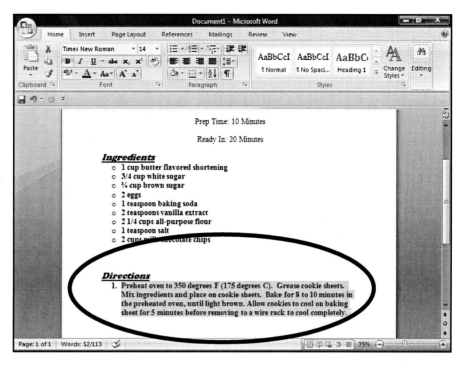

Step 2:
Click the
HOME tab.

Step 3:
Click on the
NUMBER
button's arrow.

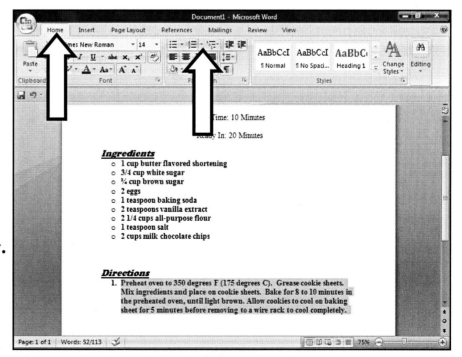

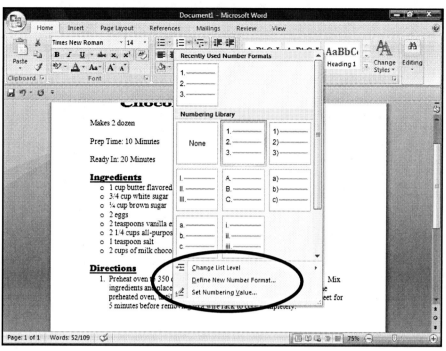

Step 4: Click on one of the advanced options located at the bottom of the Number screen.

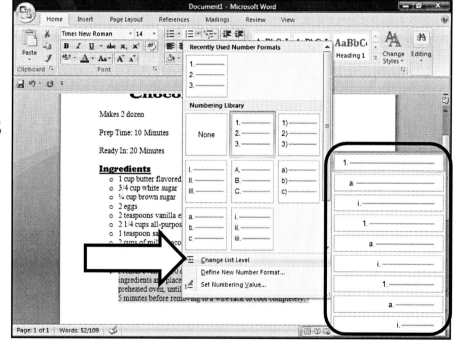

The CHANGE LIST LEVEL option.

The NEW NUMBER FORMAT SCREEN.

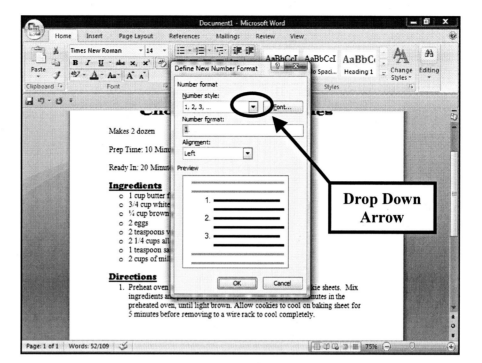

The Drop Down List.

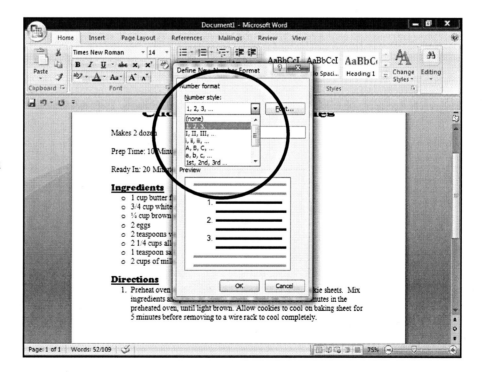

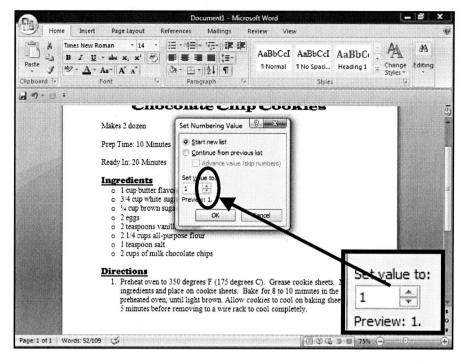

The SET NUMBERING VALUE screen.

Up and Down arrows shown.

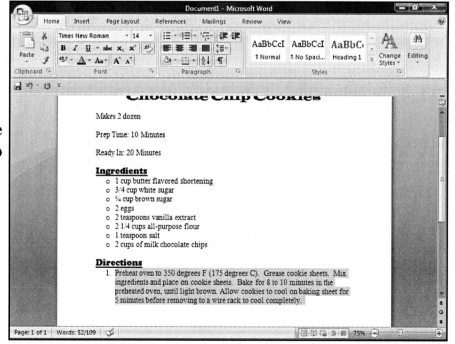

**Step 5:
Click anywhere on the screen to un-highlight your work.**

Chapter 8: Bullets & Numbers

Section 22: Editing Numbering (Adding Additional Numbers)

How Do I Add Additional Numbers to an Existing List?

The following section will address the topic of adding *additional* numbers to a list that has already been numbered. For example, the current example has a numbered list of cooking directions. The problem is that the computer looked at the list of directions and "grouped" them all together. When you numbered the list, the computer numbered the entire list "1." Take a closer look at this list; it can be broken down into five different steps. By following a few steps, you can number each direction. Click the left mouse button one time in front of the direction you want to number "2." In this example, click in front of "Grease cookie sheets." The blinking cursor will appear. Press the Enter key one time. "Grease cookie sheets" will move down one line and will be numbered "2." Repeat the process to add additional numbers.

Add Additional Numbers to an Existing List: Step by Step Instructions

1. **Click in front of the text you want to number.**
2. **Press Enter key on the keyboard.**
3. **Repeat Steps 1 and 2 to add additional numbers until your list is complete.**

Chapter 8: Bullets & Numbers

Add Additional Numbers to an Existing List: Visual Guide

Step 1:
Click in front of the word "Grease."

Step 2:
Press the Enter key on the keyboard.

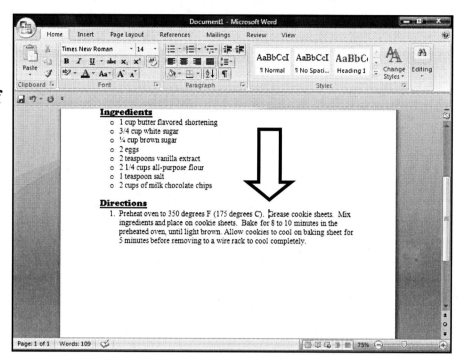

The direction "Grease Cookie Sheet" will move down one line and be numbered "2."

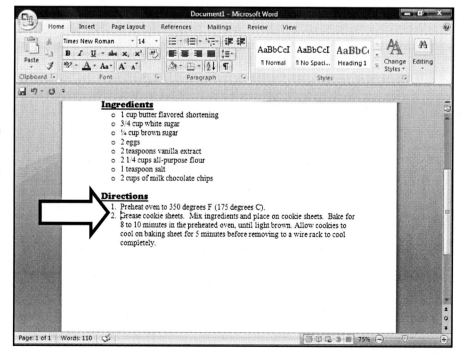

Chapter 8: Bullets & Numbers

Click in front of the word "Mix" and press the Enter key.

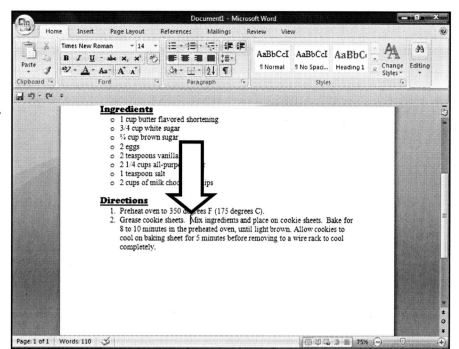

The direction "Mix ingredients…" will move down one line and be numbered "3."

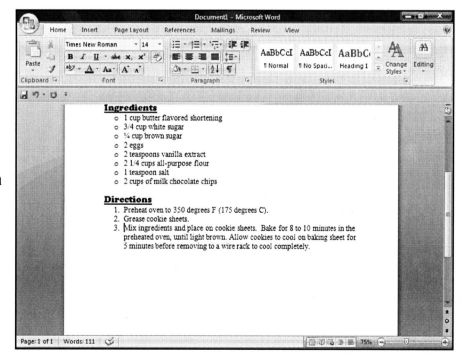

Click in front of the word "Bake" and press the Enter key.

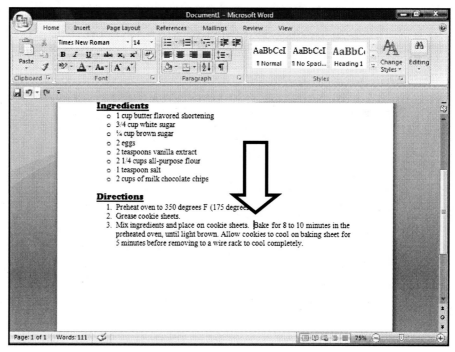

The direction "Bake for 8 to 10…" will move down one line and be numbered "4."

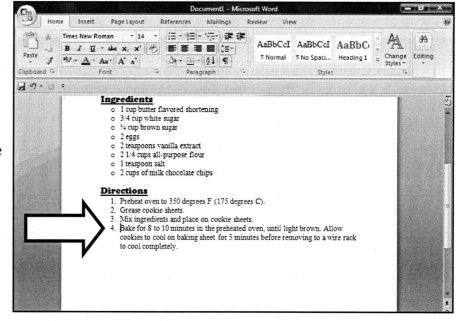

Click in front of the word "Allow" and press the Enter key.

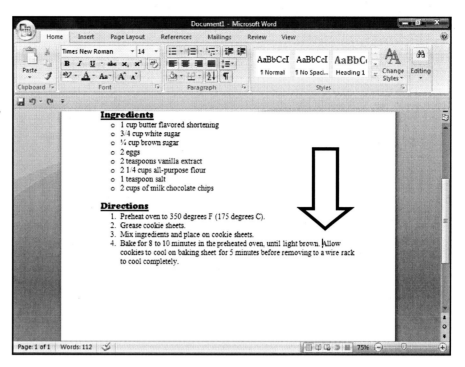

The direction "Allow cookies…" will move down one line and be numbered "5."

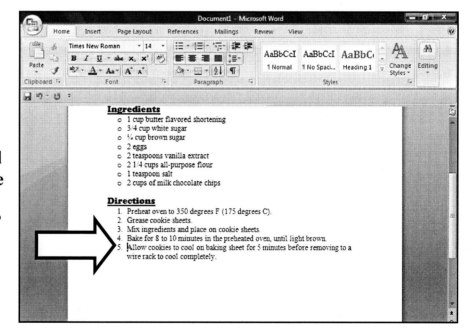

Chapter 8: Bullets & Numbers

How Do I Add New Items to a Numbered List?

To add a new item to a numbered list, first decide where in the list you want to add the item. Do want the new item to be at the top of the list, in the middle, or at the end? Place your blinking cursor at the end (to the right of) the line which should precede the new item, and press the Enter key on the keyboard. The computer will move your blinking cursor down one line, will insert a blank line, and will automatically insert a number, in sequence, for the item. Type the new item in the blank line. Every time you hit the Enter key, when the blinking cursor is at the end of a numbered line, the computer will move your cursor down to the next line and insert a new number.

NOTE: To stop a numbered list from continuing, move your blinking cursor to the end of the last item in the list and hit the Enter key on your keyboard twice. This will move your cursor down to the next line and cease the numbering formatting.

Adding New Items to a Numbered List: Step by Step Instructions

1. Place the blinking cursor at the end (to the right of) an item in the numbered list.
2. Press the Enter key on the keyboard.
   - Pressing the Enter key inserts a numbered blank line directly below the item where your blinking cursor is positioned.
3. Type your new item.

Adding New Items to a Numbered List: Visual Guide

**Step 1:
Place the blinking cursor at the end (to the right of) an item in the numbered list.**

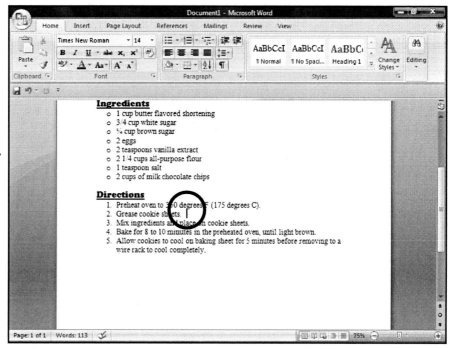

**Step 2:
Press the Enter key.**

A numbered blank space will be inserted just below the previous line.

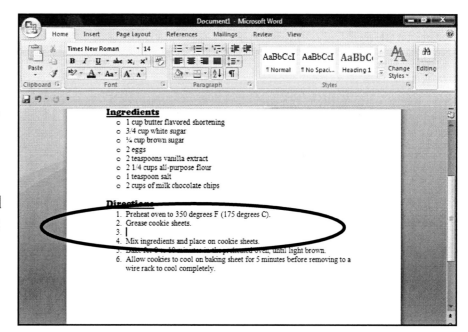

Step 3:
Type the new list item "Place all ingredients into a large bowl."

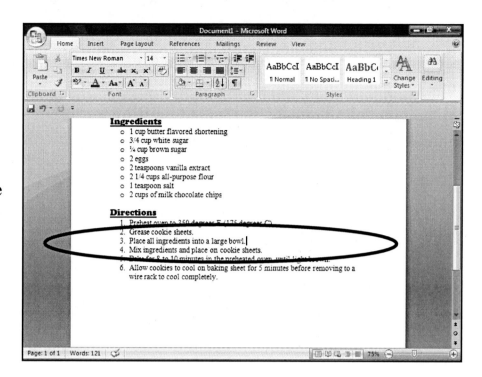

Chapter 9

Page Borders

What You Will Learn in this Chapter
✓ Placing a border around an entire page
✓ Changing the appearance of your border
✓ Adding artwork to your border

Chapter 9: Page Borders

Section 23: Adding a Border to an Entire Page

Placing Page Borders Around Documents

Adding a border around the text can add a nice finishing touch to a document. Since borders are placed in the margins of a document, they can help make work look more complete and organized without affecting the text. Borders can be simple lines, have a three-dimensional shadow, or even be made up of pictures.

NOTE: If you add a page border and then add additional pages to your document, Microsoft Word will automatically place the same border on each new page.

To add page borders to your recipe example, click on the PAGE LAYOUT tab. In the PAGE BACKGROUND section of the Page Layout ribbon, click the PAGE BORDERS option. The Borders and Shading screen will be displayed. Located at the top of this screen are three tabs -- BORDERS, PAGE BORDERS, and SHADING. The first tab, BORDERS, provides the option to place borders around specific sections of text. The second tab, PAGE BORDERS, provides the option of putting borders around the entire page. The third tab, SHADING, adds blocks of color to the document's background.

For this example, click PAGE BORDERS tab. The Page Border options will be displayed. There are five styles of borders listed on the left side of the Borders and Shading Screen. The choices are: None, Box, Shadow, 3-D, and Custom. Choose the style of border you want; in this example click on the option Shadow. A successful click will place a blue border (highlight) around the option.

NOTE: When you are practicing, select the remaining border options to see the types of borders Box, 3-D, and Custom will create. The steps to select any of the five border types are very similar.

After you have chosen the style of border (shadow), look at the center column of the Borders and Shading options screen. The center column contains four options to customize your new border -- STYLE, COLOR, WIDTH, and ART.

The STYLE option enables you to change the style of line used in your border. You can select dashed, double lined, squiggly, etc.

The COLOR option enables you to change the color of the border. Borders that are blue, red, green, etc. make striking contrasts to a plain white piece of paper.

The WIDTH option enables you to change the thickness of the border. Line thickness is measured in points. The larger the point, the thicker the line.

The fourth customization, ART, enables you to insert pictures for your border. The picture options are provided by Microsoft Word. If you choose to use the option ART, sometimes the categories Style and Color become invalid, depending on the border you choose. Some of the pictures in the ART category cannot be customized.

The next step in customizing your document border is to change the thickness of the line. Click on the drop down arrow below the WIDTH option to view a list of line thicknesses. Click on the thickness you want. The list will close, and your choice will be displayed in the Width options input box. Follow the same steps for the Color option. Click on the drop down arrow below the COLOR option to display a palette of colors. Click on the color you want. The list will close and your choice will be displayed in the Color options input box. When you are happy with your customizations, you can apply all your changes by clicking the OK button located on the bottom right of the screen.

Chapter 9: Page Borders

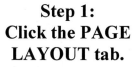

NOTE: Be creative and curious in this section. There are hundreds of different border options available. Have some fun trying various options.

Adding a Page Border: *Step by Step Instructions*

1. **Click the PAGE LAYOUT tab.**
2. **Click the PAGE BORDERS option.**
   - **The Borders and Shading options screen will appear.**
3. **Click the PAGE BORDER tab.**
4. **Select the Border Setting (left side of the options screen).**
5. **Select the Style.**
6. **Click on the drop down arrow next to the WIDTH Option.**
7. **Click on the border width you want to use.**
8. **Click on the drop down arrow below the COLOR Option.**
9. **Click on the color you want to use.**
10. **Click the OK button.**

Adding a Page Border: *Visual Guide*

Step 1:
Click the PAGE LAYOUT tab.

Step 2:
Click the PAGE BORDERS option.

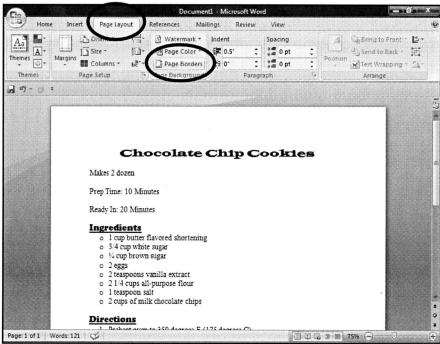

Chapter 9: Page Borders

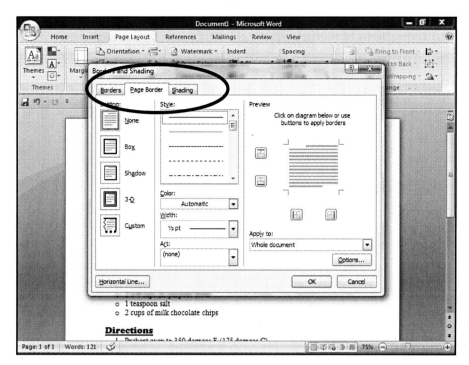

Step 3:
Click the PAGE
BORDER tab.

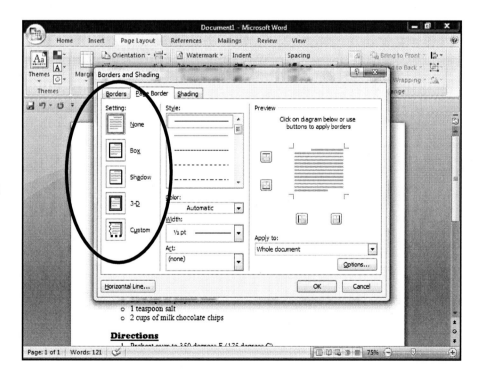

Step 4:
Click on the
SETTING you
want.

Step 5:
Click on the
STYLE of line
you want.

Step 6:
Click on the
drop down
arrow next to
the WIDTH
option.

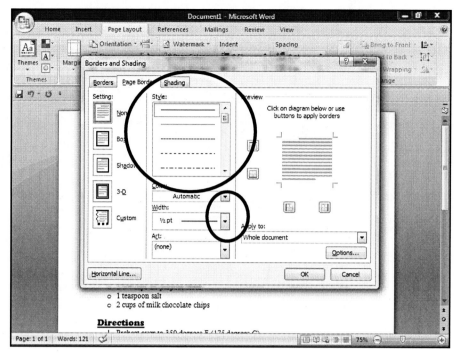

Step 7:
Click on border
width you
desire.

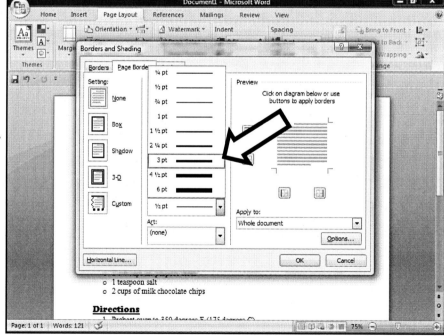

Chapter 9: Page Borders

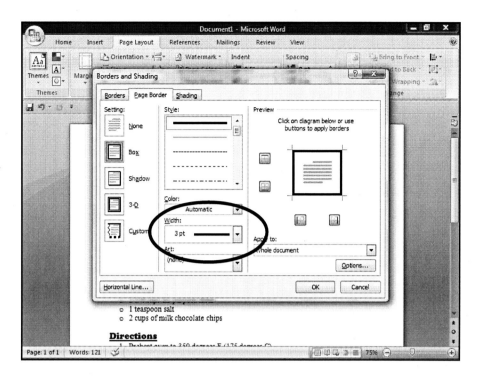

Your selection will be displayed in the Width Input box.

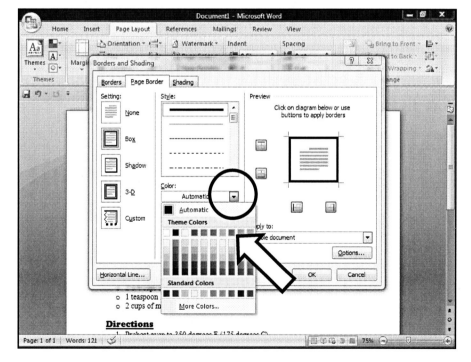

Step 8:
Click on the drop down arrow below the COLOR option.

Step 9:
Click on the color you want.

Your color selection will be displayed in the color input box.

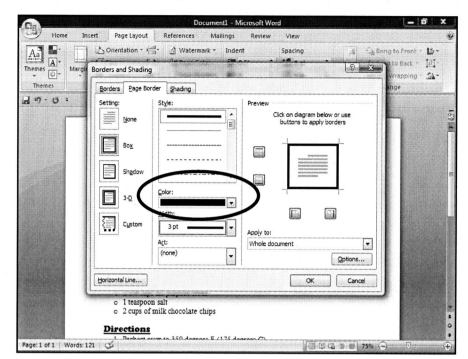

Step 10: Click the OK button to apply your border.

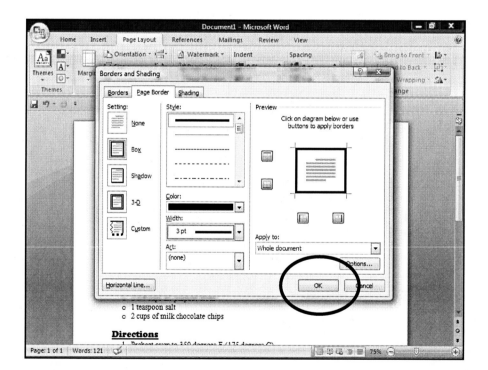

Chapter 9: Page Borders

The border has been applied.

Remember: To view the entire page, go to Print Preview.

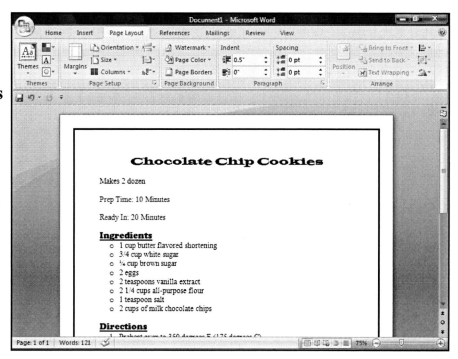

Chapter 9: Page Borders

Chapter 10

Copying, Cutting & Pasting

What You Will Learn in this Chapter
- ✓ The terms *copy*, *cut*, and *paste*
- ✓ Copying and Pasting text
- ✓ Cutting and Pasting text

Chapter 10: Copying, Cutting & Pasting

Section 24: Copying and Pasting

What is Copying and Pasting?

Copying and Pasting is a process that lets you make a copy of text located in one area of your document and paste it in another. The computer places the copy into a temporary holding area called the Clipboard. When you've chosen where you want the copied text inserted, the computer places it into the new area.

Have you ever written a long and involved paper only to realize when you were finished that your paragraphs needed to be reorganized or the order of your topics needed to be changed? Before the days of the Copy and Paste function, you would have had to rewrite the entire paper. Now, reorganizing paragraphs, sections, and even entire documents can be accomplished in just a few steps. Microsoft Word lets you make exact copies of text or pictures in a document and place the copies in additional locations. This process is referred to as Copying and Pasting

Getting Ready to Practice Copying and Pasting

To practice Copying and Pasting, open a new blank document by using the Office menu. Click the OFFICE button, and then click the NEW option. When the new screen is displayed, click the CREATE button. A new blank document will open.

After you have opened a new blank document, begin typing an attendance list for a group meeting. The title will be "Group Meetings" and the first meeting was on January 10. The following people attended the meeting: John Doe, Jane Smith, Jim Brown, Amy Tan, Betty Jones, Catherine Wade, Larry Scotch, and Brian Katz. Type this information in so it resembles the following example.

Chapter 10: Copying, Cutting & Pasting

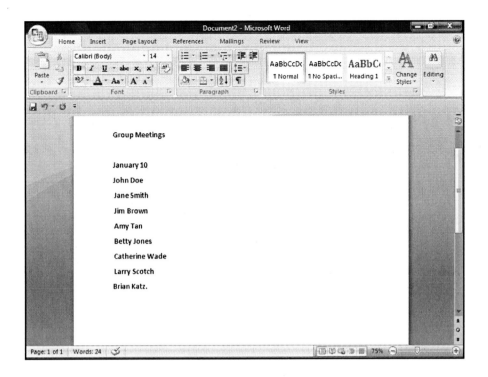

The Process of Copying and Pasting

Next, assume that you had another meeting and the same people attend. Instead of re-typing all the names, you will use the Copy and Paste function. First, type the second meeting date, February 28, two lines below Brian Katz.

Hint: To move the blinking cursor down two lines below Brian Katz, click after Brian Katz's name. When the blinking cursor has been placed after Brain Katz's name, press the Enter key on the keyboard twice.

You are now going to copy the list of people from the January 10th meeting and paste it below the February 28th meeting date. To copy the list of names, first highlight the list. After the names have been highlighted, click the HOME tab. Move the mouse arrow on top of the CLIPBOARD section of the Clipboard ribbon, and click on the small picture of the two pieces of paper. The two pieces of paper represent the COPY option. It will seem like nothing happened, but the computer has made a copy of the highlighted text. The next step is to instruct the computer where to place the copied text. To do this, click your mouse to the right of February 28. The blinking cursor should now be blinking at the end of the line after 28. Press the Enter key on the keyboard one time to move your blinking cursor down one line. The cursor is now located at the point where you want to put the copied list. Move the mouse arrow back to the Clipboard section of the Home ribbon, and click on the picture of the clipboard. The clipboard represents the Paste Option. The list of names will appear where the blinking cursor was located, just below February 10th. The process you have just finished is called Copying and Pasting.

Now move the cursor down to the next line, and type the next meeting date: June 20. Assume the same people attended this meeting. Copy and paste the list of names a second time by following the same steps.

Now move the cursor down to the next line, and type the next meeting date: April 15. Assume that the same people attended this meeting. Copy and paste the list of names again by following the same steps.

Copying and Pasting: Step by Step Instructions
1. **Highlight the text you want to copy.**
2. **Click the Home tab.**
3. **Click the picture of the two pieces of paper (COPY).**
4. **Place your blinking cursor where you want the copied text to be inserted.**
5. **Click the clipboard symbol (PASTE).**
    *   **The copied text will be pasted where the cursor was positioned.**
6. **Move your cursor down the page and type in the next meeting date.**
7. **Highlight the text you want to copy.**
8. **Click the picture of the two pieces of paper (COPY).**
9. **Place your blinking cursor where you want the copied text to be inserted.**
10. **Click the clipboard symbol (PASTE).**
    *   **The copied text will be pasted where the cursor was positioned.**
11. **Repeat Steps 1 through 5.**

Chapter 10: Copying, Cutting & Pasting

Copying and Pasting: A Visual Guide

Step 1:
Highlight the text you want to copy.

Step 2:
Click the Home tab.

Step 3:
Click the picture of the two pieces of paper (COPY).

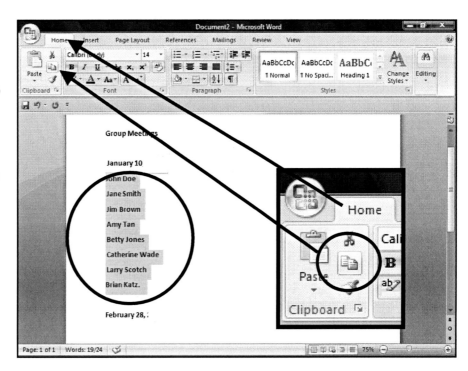

Step 4:
Place the blinking cursor where you want the copied text to be inserted.

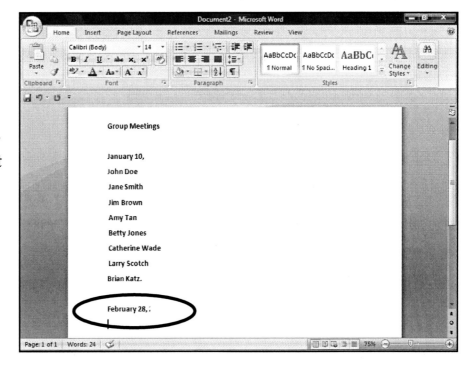

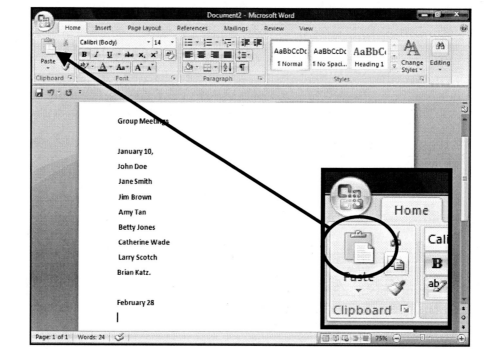

Step 5: Click the clipboard symbol (PASTE).

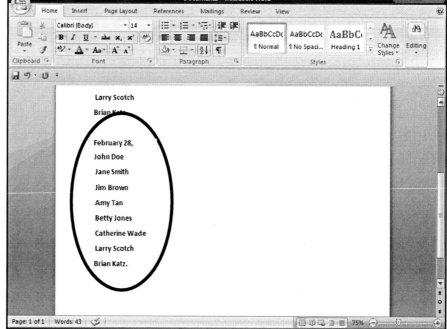

The copied text will be pasted where the blinking cursor was positioned.

**Step 6:
Move your
blinking cursor
down the page
and type:
June 20.**

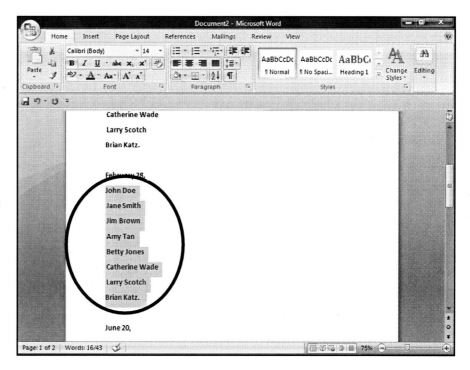

**Step 7:
Highlight the
text you want to
copy.**

Step 8:
Click the picture of the two pieces of paper (COPY).

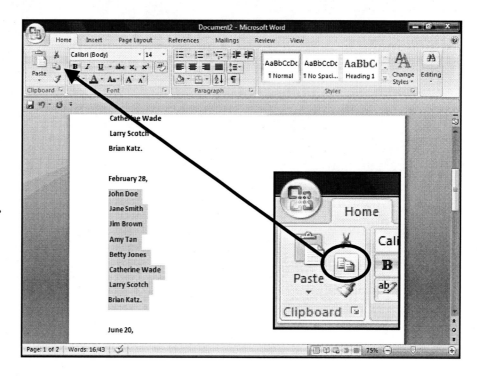

Step 9:
Place the blinking cursor under June 20.

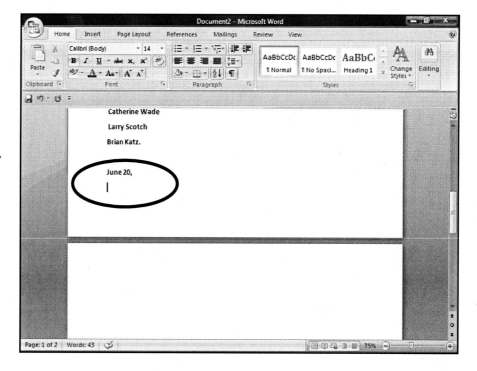

Step 10: Click on the clipboard symbol (PASTE).

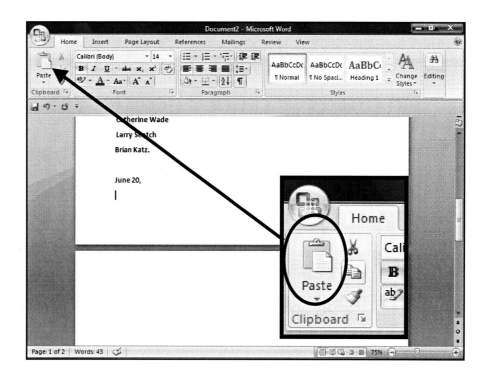

The copied text will be pasted where the blinking cursor was positioned.

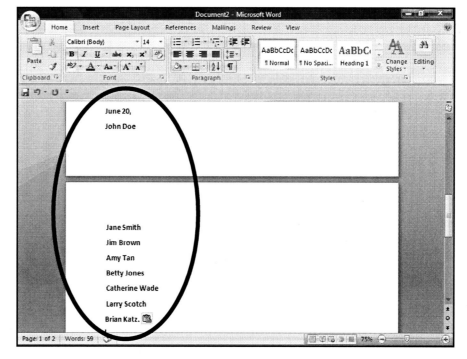

Chapter 10: Copying, Cutting & Pasting

Step 11:
Move your blinking cursor down the page and type:
April 15.

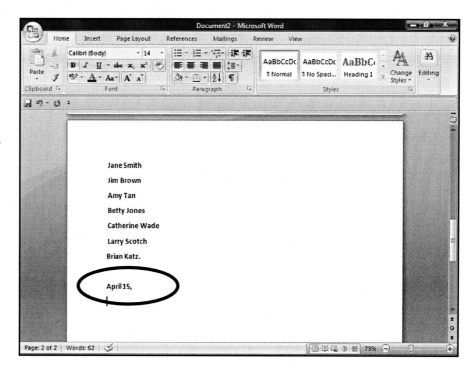

Step 12:
Highlight the text you want to copy.

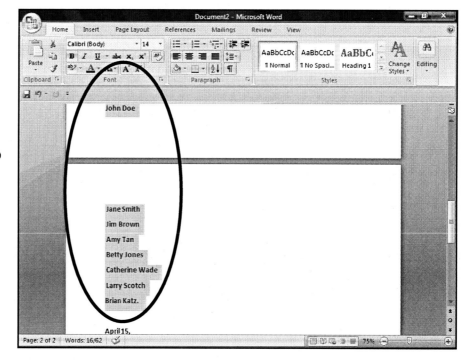

**Step 13:
Click the
picture of the
two pieces of
paper (COPY).**

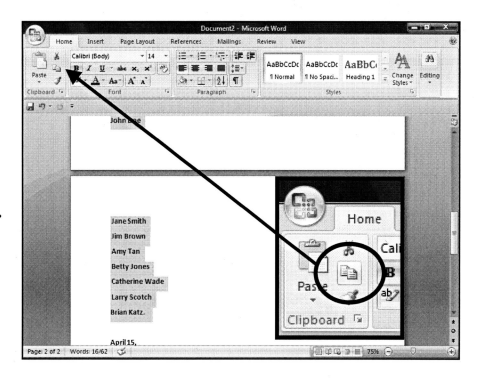

**Step 14:
Place the
blinking cursor
under April 15.**

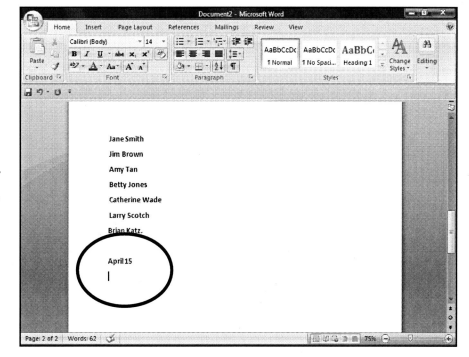

**Step 15:
Click the
clipboard
symbol.
(PASTE)**

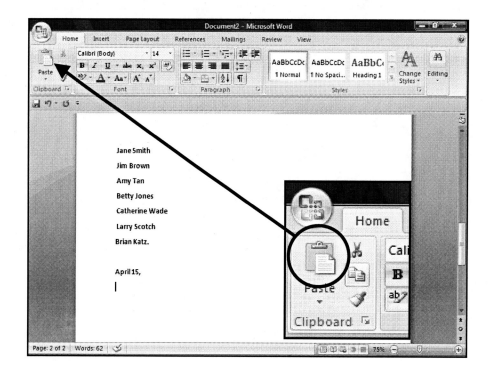

**The copied text
will be pasted
where the
blinking cursor
was located.**

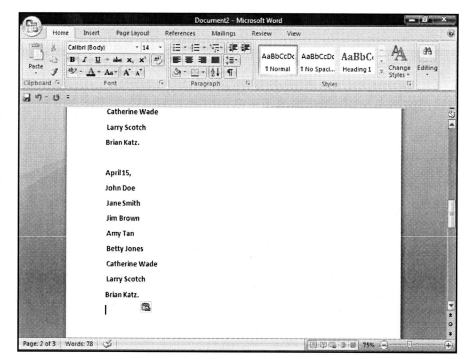

Chapter 10: Copying, Cutting & Pasting

Section 25: Cutting & Pasting

Introducing Cutting & Pasting

Cutting and Pasting is a process in which you *remove* text from a location in your document. The computer places the text into a temporary holding spot called your Clipboard. When you chose where you want the cut text inserted, the computer places it into the new area.

To practice Cutting and Pasting, continue to use the meeting list example you created in the Copy and Paste section of this book. Notice that the meeting dates are out of order. The list begins with January and February meetings and then jumps to June before listing the April meeting. Using the cut and paste function, you will be able to remove (cut) the June meeting and place (paste) it in the proper order, by date, on the page.

The Cut and Paste Process

Highlight the text you want to remove. In this example, highlight the April date and the list of attendees at the April meeting. Once the text is highlighted, click the HOME tab, move the mouse arrow on top of the CLIPBOARD section of the Home ribbon, and click on the picture of the scissors. The scissors represent the CUT option. The highlighted text will disappear from the screen. It is now stored in your clipboard. Next, position the blinking cursor where you want the "removed" text to be placed. Position the mouse arrow on the blank line below the last name of the person attending the February meeting, and click your left mouse button. The blinking cursor will appear beneath the last name of the person attending the February meeting. Press the Enter key on your keyboard to leave one blank line between your cursor and the February meeting. Finally, click on the picture of the clipboard (PASTE) located on the Clipboard section of the Home ribbon. A successful click will place (paste) the "removed" text at the point where your blinking cursor is located. You have successfully completed the Cut and Paste process.

Chapter 10: Copying, Cutting & Pasting

Cutting and Pasting: Step by Step Instructions

1. Highlight the text you want to cut (remove).
2. Click the HOME tab.
3. Click the picture of the scissors (Cut).
   - The text will be removed from the screen.
4. Position the blinking cursor where you want to place the cut text.
5. Press the Enter key to add additional spaces for the text. (This step is optional. You can add extra spaces after placing the text.)
6. Click the picture of the clipboard (Paste).
   - The Cut text will reappear where the blinking cursor was located.

Cutting and Pasting: Visual Guide

**Step 1:
Highlight the
text you want to
cut.**

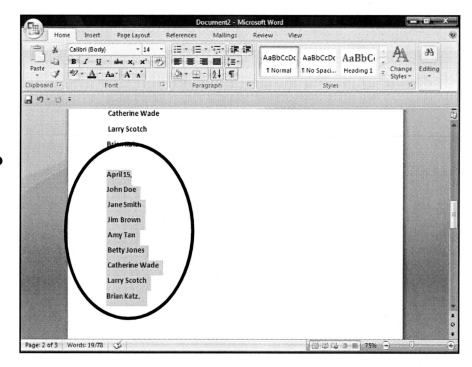

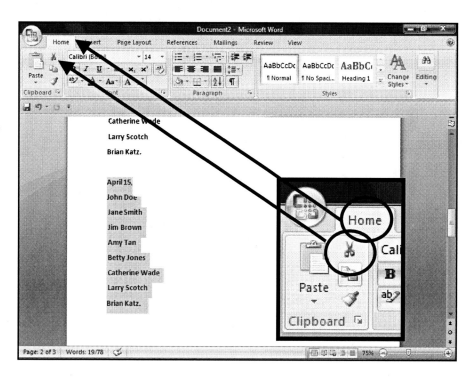

Step 2:
Click the Home tab.

Step 3:
Click the picture of the scissors (CUT).

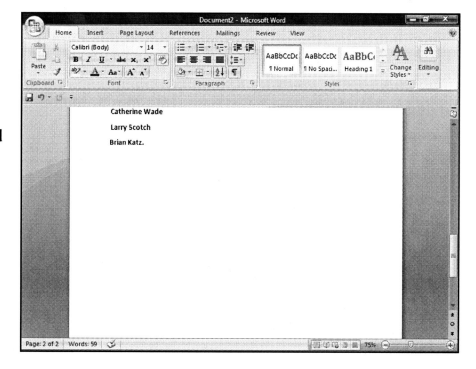

The highlighted text will be removed from the screen.

Step 4:
Place the blinking cursor where you want to place the cut text.

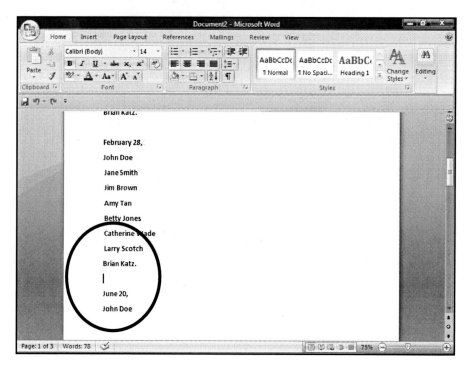

Step 5:
Use the Enter key to make some space for the text.

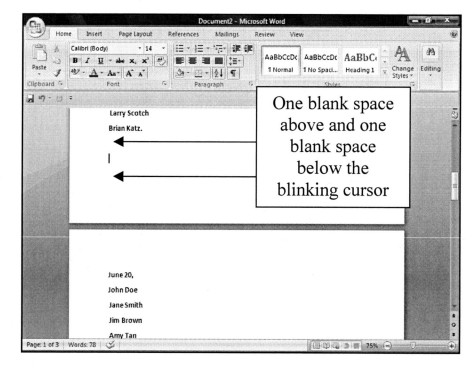

One blank space above and one blank space below the blinking cursor

Step 6:
Click the
clipboard
symbol.
(PASTE)

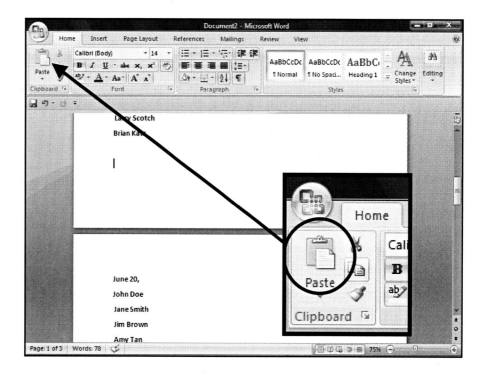

The cut text has been placed where the blinking cursor was positioned.

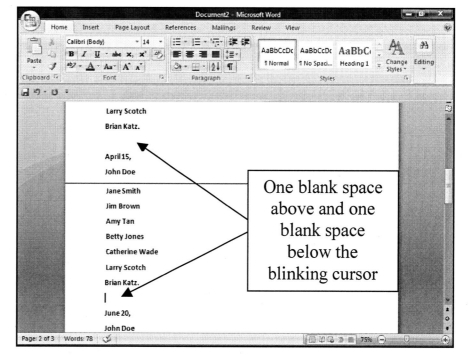

One blank space above and one blank space below the blinking cursor

Chapter 10: Copying, Cutting & Pasting

Chapter 11

Saving Your Work to a Flash Drive

What You Will Learn in this Chapter
- ✓ The term "flash drive"
- ✓ The advantages of saving your work to a flash drive
- ✓ Saving your work to a flash drive

Chapter 11: Saving Your Work to a Flash Drive

Section 26: Saving Your Work on a Flash Drive

What is Saving?

REMEMBER: "Saving" is the process of instructing the computer to store your document until you decide to delete it. Any information that is not saved will be lost if the computer loses power, the program freezes, or you unintentionally close the document.

What is a Flash Drive?

A Flash Drive is a very popular portable storage device. Flash drives are small, easy to use, durable devices which can store a large amount of information. Flash drives store information and allow information to be easily transferred from one computer to another. Flash drives are small enough to be carried in a pocket or be attached to a keychain. In the picture to the right, you can see a flash drive placed next to a quarter to show you that, in comparison to CDs and DVDs, flash drives are very small.

To use a flash drive, remove the cover protecting the flash drive's plug. Plug the drive into the USB port (socket) in your computer. Now, you can transfer information from the computer to the flash drive.

Flash drives are also called pen drives, thumb drives, key drives, USB Drives, and an assortment of other names.

What are the Advantages of Using a Flash Drive?

Saving your work to a flash drive allows you to take your files with you wherever you go. Whether you need to transport your work from home to your place of employment, to a friend's house, or take it with you on vacation, flash drives provide a simple solution. You can also use flash drives to back up important files already saved to your computer's hard drive.

Revisiting the Chocolate Chip Cookie Recipe

If the Chocolate Chip Recipe is still open on your computer, use that document in the next exercise. But, if the recipe has been closed or lost, open a new blank document and type the following:

– – – – – – – – – – – – – – – –

Chocolate Chip Cookies

Makes 2 dozen
Prep Time: 10 minutes
Ready in: 20 minutes

Ingredients
1 cup butter flavored shortening
¾ cup white sugar
2 eggs
2 teaspoons vanilla extract
2 ¼ cups all-purpose flower
1 teaspoon salt

Directions
Preheat oven to 350 degrees F (175 degrees C). Grease cookie sheets. Mix the ingredients and place on the cookie sheets. Bake for 8 to 10 minutes in the preheated oven, until light brown. Allow cookies to cool on baking sheet for 5 minutes before removing to a wire rack to cool completely.

Chapter 11: Saving Your Work to a Flash Drive

Finished Results

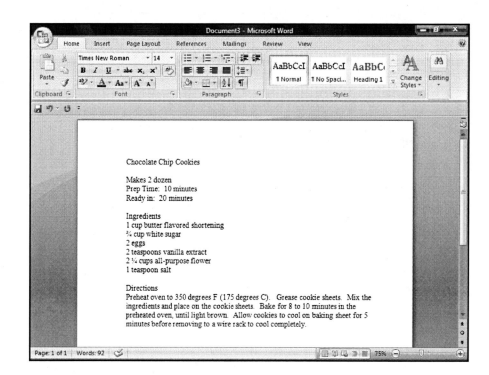

The Process of Saving Your Work to a Flash Drive

The first step in saving your work to a flash drive is to insert the flash drive into the computer's USB port. After inserting the flash drive, click on the OFFICE button in the upper left corner of your recipe window. Click on the option SAVE AS. The "Save As" screen will appear. "Save As" enables you to save your work to your computer or your flash drive. To save your work to a flash drive, you have to tell the computer two things: (1) where you want to save your work and (2) what you want to name your file.

First, tell the computer where you want to save your work. In the upper left corner of the "Save As" screen you will see the words "Favorite Links." Located below this title is a list of the most popular places to save your document. To save your document to a flash drive, click on the COMPUTER link. After clicking on the "Computer" link, look at the center of the Save As screen. Several options will be listed. One of the options will be the CD or DVD drive, usually labeled as drive "D" or "F." Another option will be your computer's hard drive represented by the Local "C" drive. There may be other drives, but at least one option will be the flash drive you inserted. The flash drive will either be labeled "Removable Disk" or possibly by the name of company that designed the flash drive. In either case it will probably be labeled as drive "E" or "F." In the example in the book, the flash drive is

Chapter 11: Saving Your Work to a Flash Drive

labeled REMOVABLE DRIVE (F:). Double click on the flash drive, and the name of the flash drive will be displayed in the long white text box near the top of the SAVE AS screen. You have just successfully informed your computer where you would like to save your work.

The next step is to tell the computer what you would like to name your document. To assign a name, look near the bottom of the "Save As" screen. You will see the words FILE NAME. Directly to the right of the words "File Name" is a white input box where you can type in the name you chose. Click in the file name box one time with the left mouse button. Any text inside the file name input box will turn blue. Press either the Delete key or the Backspace key to erase anything in the input box. Once everything has been erased from the input box, type a descriptive name for your work. In this example, name the recipe "Cookie Recipe." Once you have chosen a location, the flash drive, and a name, you are ready to click the Save button. The SAVE button is in the lower right corner of the Save As screen. Place your mouse arrow on the SAVE button, and click once with your left mouse button. Congratulations, the cookie recipe has been saved to a flash drive!

Saving Your Work to a Flash Drive: Step by Step Instructions
1. **Insert a flash drive into the computer's USB port.**
2. **Click the OFFICE button located in the upper left corner of the window.**
3. **Click the SAVE AS option.**
   - **The Save As screen will appear.**
4. **Click the COMPUTER link.**
5. **Click REMOVABLE DISK.**
6. **Click in the FILE NAME box once with the left mouse button.**
7. **Press either the Delete key or the Backspace key to erase anything in the input box.**
8. **Type a descriptive name for your file.**
   - **The file name may not include periods, colons, semicolons, or mathematical operators, e.g. the plus and minus signs).**
9. **Click the SAVE button in the lower right corner of the "Save As" screen.**

Chapter 11: Saving Your Work to a Flash Drive

Saving Your Work to a Flash Drive: Visual Guide

Step 1:
Insert a flash drive into the computer's UHB port.

Step 2:
Click the OFFICE button.

Step 3:
Click the SAVE AS option.

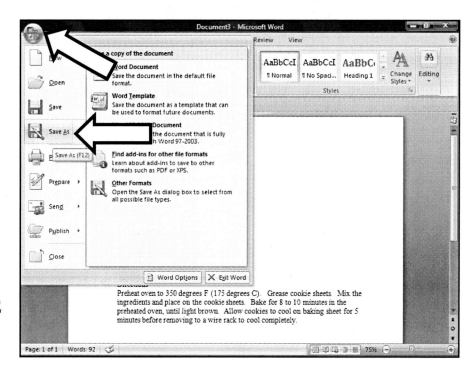

Step 4:
Click the COMPUTER link.

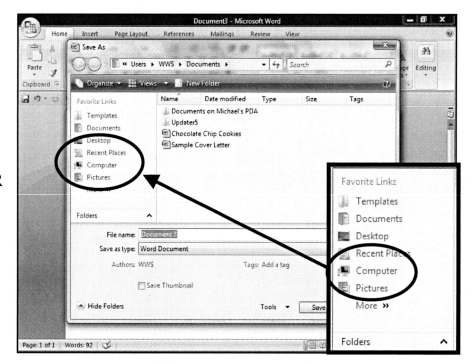

**Step 5:
Click
REMOVABLE
DISK.**

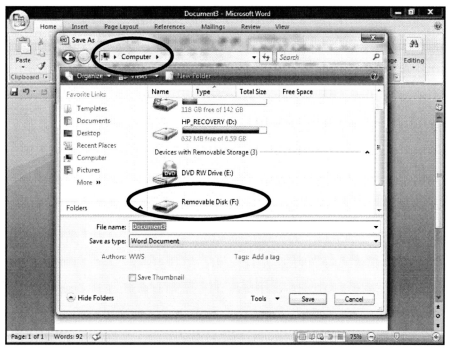

**You have just
successfully told
the computer
where you want
to save your
recipe.**

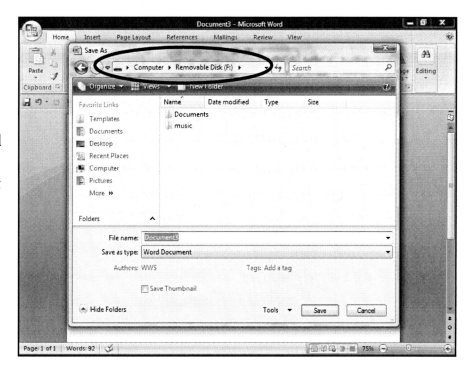

Step 6:
Click in the File Name box.

Step 7:
Erase the contents of the File Name box.

Step 8:
Type a new name for your recipe.

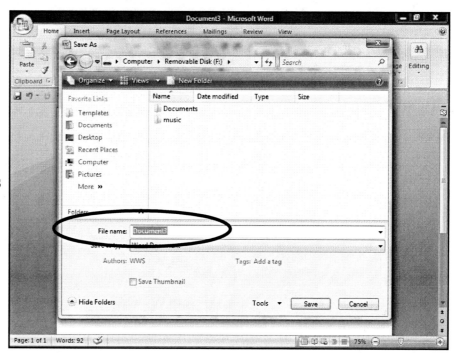

Step 9:
Click the SAVE button.

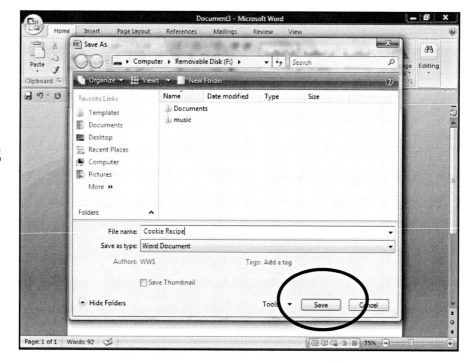

Chapter 11: Saving Your Work to a Flash Drive

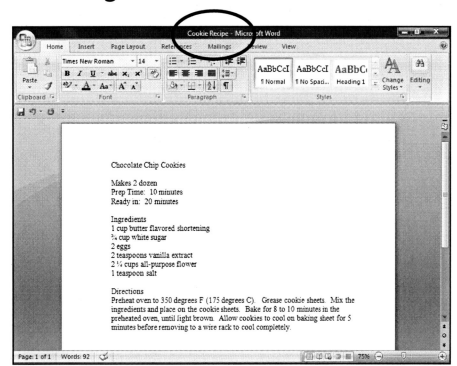

Your recipe is now safely saved to a flash drive.

Section 27: Removing a Flash Drive from the Computer

Proper Removal of Flash Drives

When you are finished using the Flash Drive, it is very important that you take the proper steps to remove the Flash Drive from the computer. Do not just pull the Flash Drive out of the USB port. This could cause unwanted problems. To remove a Flash Drive from the computer, look in the lower right corner of the computer screen. The lower right corner of the taskbar contains a series of tiny icons, known as the Notification Area. (This area used to be called the System Tray.) Within the Notification Area is an icon that resembles a small plug. When the Flash Drive is inserted into the computer, the icon of the small plug will have a green checkmark next to it. If you cannot figure out which tiny icon is the "small plug," place your mouse arrow on each of the tiny icons, without clicking, and a short description will appear next to the icon. The "small plug" icon will display the description "Safely Remove Hardware." Once you have located the "small plug" icon, place your mouse arrow on the

icon and double click. A new screen will appear. The title bar will read
"Safely Remove Hardware." A STOP button is located on the lower right side
of the screen. Click the STOP button. A confirmation screen will appear.
Click the OK button. You can now safely remove the Flash Drive from the
USB port.

Note: Sometimes all of the icons in the Notification Area will not be
displayed. To view all of the icons, click on the small arrow located just to the
left of the Notification Area.

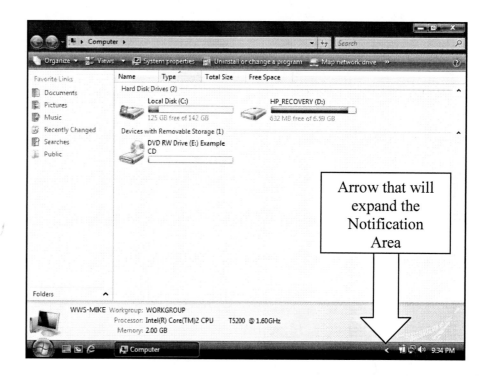

Removing a Flash Drive: Step by Step Instructions
   1. **Locate the "small Plug" icon.**
   2. **Double click on the "Small Plug" icon.**
   3. **Click the STOP button.**
   4. **Click the OK button.**

Removing a Flash Drive: Visual Guide

Step 1: Locate the "Small plug" icon.

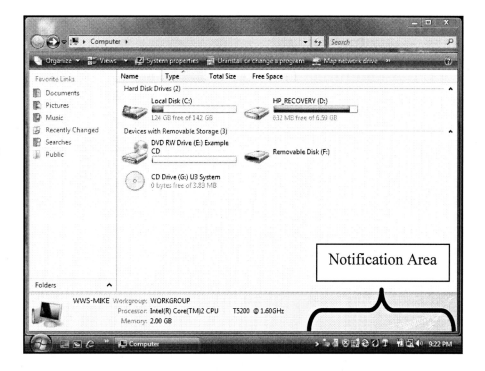

If needed: Place the mouse arrow on the icons to see the descriptions.

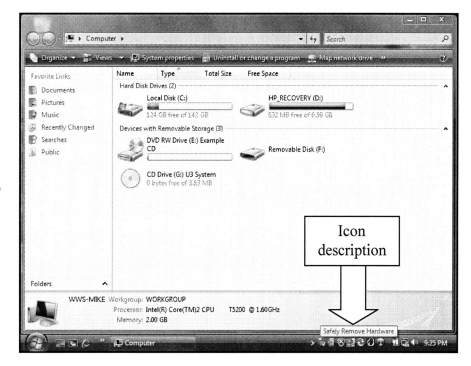

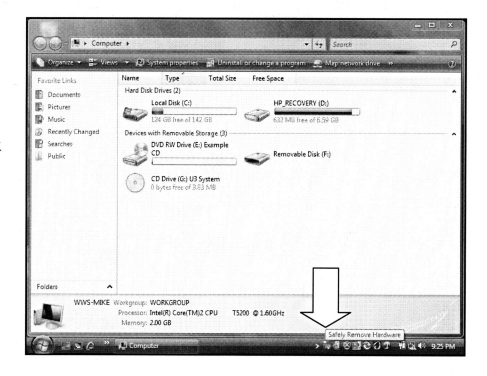

Step 2:
Double click
the "Small
Plug" icon.

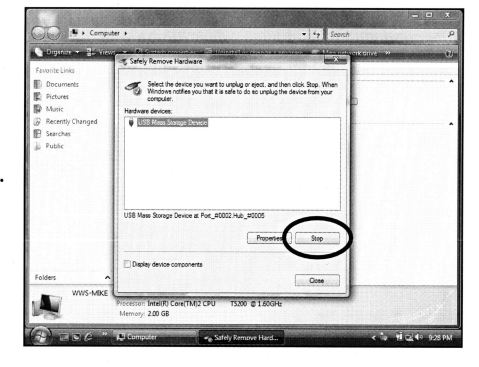

Step 3:
Click the
STOP button.

Step 4:
Click the OK button.

Step 5:
Remove the Flash Drive from the computer.

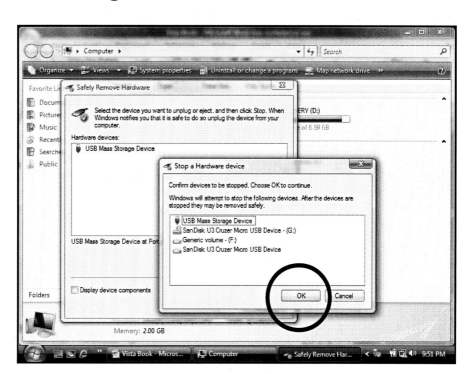

Chapter 11: Saving Your Work to a Flash Drive

Chapter 12

Shortcuts

What You Will Learn in this Chapter
- ✓ The Control Keys
- ✓ Using the Control Keys

Chapter 12: Shortcuts

Section 28: The Control Keys

What Are The Control Keys Used For?

So far you've learned how to edit and/or format your work using the tabs and ribbons. There is also a second option. The second way to edit or format your work is through the "Control Key" functions. The Control Keys give you the ability to make editing/formatting selections without taking your hands off the keyboard. The Control Key options can be selected by holding down the Control key (Ctrl) on the keyboard and pressing a second key on the keyboard at the same time. Different combinations will produce different results. For example, holding down the Control (Ctrl) key while pressing the letter "C" will perform the "Copy" function. Holding down the Control (Ctrl) key while pressing the letter "S" will "Save" your work.

For your convenience, a list of these Control key functions is listed below. You can also view these keyboard combinations by placing the mouse arrow on top of any function located on a ribbon. If you click the HOME tab and place the mouse arrow on top of any function of the Home ribbon, a light blue tip box will appear just below the mouse arrow. The light blue tip box will display a short description of the function the mouse arrow is currently positioned on as well as the combination keys that can be used to perform that function. For example, placing the mouse arrow on top of the picture of the scissors on the Home ribbon will display "CUT (CTRL + X)" in a light blue box just below the mouse arrow, indicating that pressing the Control key down at the same time as the "X" key will perform the cut function on any highlighted text. If no combination keys are listed next to an option, that function does not have a control key combination.

The Control key can be pressed simultaneously with a variety of other keys to perform many helpful tasks.

Chapter 12: Shortcuts

 Hint: The Control keys are another option available to computer users. You do not have to use them. Use whichever method seems the easiest for you. Some people use the ribbons, some people use control keys, and some people use a combination. It's all a matter of personal preference.

 Hint: "Control Keys" are sometime referred to as "Hot Keys."

Quick Reference Guide to the Control Keys

Control + "N" = OPENS a NEW blank document
Control + "O" = OPENS a previously saved file
Control + "S" = SAVES your work
Control + "P" = PRINTS your work
Control + "Z" = UNDOES your last action
Control + "Y" = REDOES an Undo
Control + "A" = SELECT ALL, highlights everything in the entire document
Control + "F" = FIND, enables you to search for a specific word in your Document
Control + "H" = REPLACE, enables you to change a word in your document to another word
Control + "G" = GOTO, enables you to move your cursor to a specific place in your document
Control + "C" = COPIES highlighted text
Control + "X" = CUTS highlighted text
Control + "V" = PASTES copied or cut text

Reminder: Control Key functions can be located under the various Microsoft Word Menus.

 Hint: Control + F, Control + H, and Control + G are most often used in very long documents when pinpointing a specific section or word can be difficult.

193

Chapter 12: Shortcuts

<u>Chapter 13</u>

Addressing Envelopes

What You Will Learn in this Chapter
- ✓ Printing an address on a standard business size envelope
- ✓ Printing an address on different sized envelopes

Chapter 13: Addressing Envelopes

Section 29: Addressing Envelopes

The Process of Addressing Envelopes

One of the most popular features available to Microsoft Word users is the ability to print mailing addresses directly onto envelopes. This option is located on the Mailings ribbon. Click on the MAILINGS tab. The Mailings ribbon will be displayed. Find the CREATE portion of the ribbon. Place the mouse arrow on top of the option ENVELOPES and click once. The Envelopes and Labels option screen will appear.

Located at the top of the Envelopes and Labels option screen are two tabs. One tab is titled Envelopes; the other is titled Labels. To display the Envelope options, the Envelope tab must be selected. You can make sure the ENVELOPES tab is selected by clicking it one time. When the Envelopes tab has been selected, the options screen will have two input boxes displayed. The top input box is designated for the mailing address. The bottom box is for the return address. Click in the top box, and the blinking cursor will appear. Type the mailing address. After the mailing address is complete, click in the bottom box and type the return address. You are now ready to print your envelope. If you are using a standard size business envelope (4 ⅛ x 9 ½) place the envelope into the printer, and click on the PRINT button located on the bottom left side of the Envelopes and Labels screen.

Placing an Envelope into Your Printer

The way you place the envelope into your printer is determined by the type of printer you have. Some printers take envelopes vertically with the flap down. Others take the envelopes horizontally with the flaps up. Due to the differences in printers, it is a good idea to use a test envelope first. Test to see how the printer prints on the test envelope and then make the proper adjustments before putting in a good envelope.

Chapter 13: Addressing Envelopes

Using Different Size Envelopes

The size of the envelope you are using will also make a difference. If you are using an envelope that is not business standard (4 ⅛ x 9 ½) you will have to change your print settings. You can change your print settings by clicking on the OPTIONS button located at the bottom of the Envelopes option screen. When you click on the Options button, a new list of options will be displayed. The heading "Envelope Size" is located near the top of the screen. Just below this heading is an input box listing the computer's current setting for envelope size. To change this setting, click on the drop down arrow and select a new setting from the drop down list. After selecting a new size envelope, click the OK button located at the bottom of the same screen.

Addressing Envelopes: Step by Step Instructions

1. **Click the MAILINGS tab.**
2. **Find the CREATE section of the ribbon and click the ENVELOPES option.**
3. **Click the ENVELOPES tab.**
4. **Click in the Delivery Address box and type the Mailing Address.**
5. **Click in the Return Address box and type the Return Address.**
6. **Place an envelope in your printer.**
7. **Click the PRINT button.**

Chapter 13: Addressing Envelopes

Addressing Envelopes: Visual Guide

Step 1:
Click the
MAILINGS tab.

Step 2:
In the CREATE
section of the
ribbon, click on
the option
ENVELOPES.

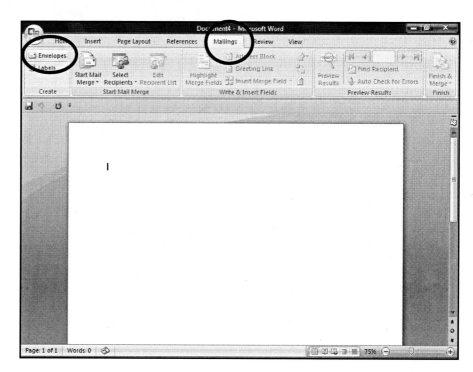

Step 3:
Click the
ENVELOPES
tab.

Step 4:
Click in the
Delivery Address
box. Type the
mailing address.

Step 5:
Click in the
Return Address
box. Type the
return address.

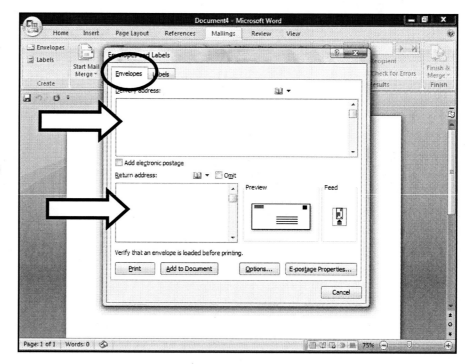

Step 6:
Place an envelope in your printer.

Step 7:
Click the PRINT button.

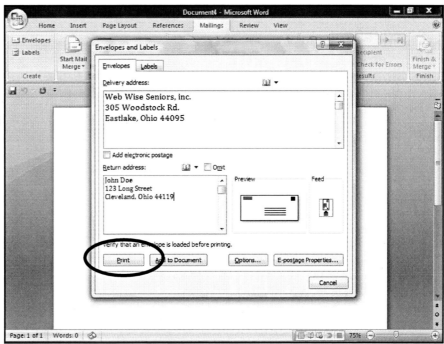

Using Different Sized Envelopes: Step by Step Instructions

1. Click the MAILINGS tab.
2. Click the ENVELOPES option.
3. Click the ENVELOPES tab.
4. Click the OPTIONS button.
5. Click on the drop down arrow located below the heading ENVELOPE SIZE.
6. Select the desired envelope size.
7. Click the OK button.
8. Perform Steps 4 through 7 in the Addressing Envelopes Instructions to finish addressing and printing the envelope.

Chapter 13: Addressing Envelopes

Using Different Sized Envelopes: Visual Guide

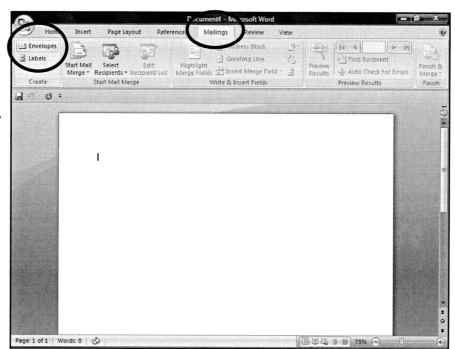

Step 1:
Click the
MAILINGS tab.

Step 2:
Click the
ENVELOPES
option.

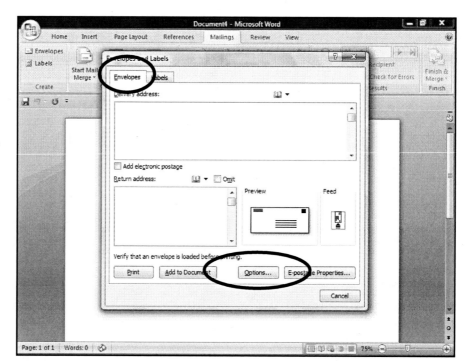

Step 3:
Click the
Envelopes tab.

Step 4:
Click the
OPTIONS
button.

Chapter 13: Addressing Envelopes

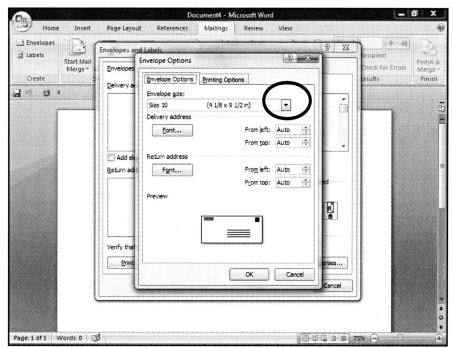

Step 5:
Click the ENVELOPE SIZE drop down arrow.

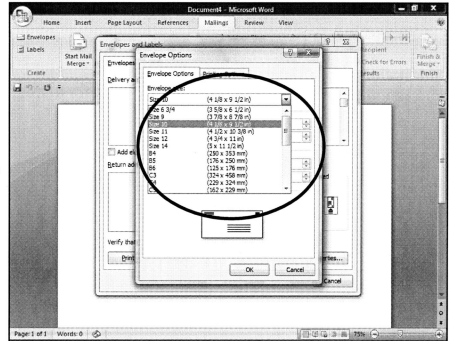

Step 6:
Click on the desired envelope size.

**Step 7:
Click the OK
button.**

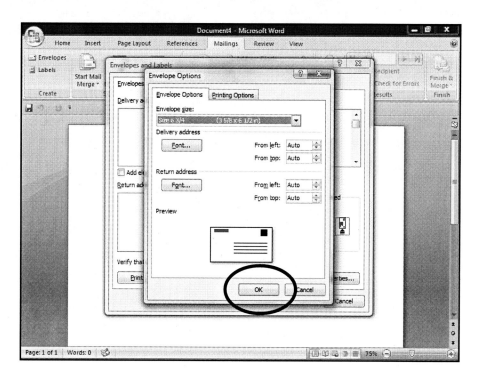

Chapter 14

Page Layout and Margins

What You Will Learn in this Chapter
- ✓ The term default
- ✓ Microsoft Word's default page settings
- ✓ Changing your page margins
- ✓ Changing your page orientation

Section 30: Default Settings

Introducing Microsoft Word's Default Page Settings

Microsoft Word is designed to start every new document with the same page layout and margins. These automatic or pre-set page settings are known as default settings. Default settings help Microsoft Word users get started more quickly and make using Word easier. You don't have to worry about setting your margins, setting your text size, what side of the page you start typing on, what type of font you want to use, etc. Microsoft Word takes care of it all.

Page Orientation (Default = Vertical)

The most important default settings can be found in the PAGE LAYOUT ribbon and include page orientation, margins, text options, page size, and paragraph alignment. PAGE ORIENTATION controls the way your page is laid out -- vertically (8 ½" x 11") or horizontally (11" x 8 ½"). The default setting for Microsoft Word documents is always vertical.

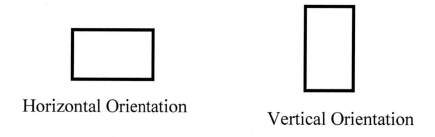

Horizontal Orientation

Vertical Orientation

Margins
(Default = 1.25" top, 1.25" bottom, 1.0" left, 1.0" right)

In the PAGE LAYOUT ribbon, MARGINS controls the distance from the edge of the paper you can type. All pages have four margins: top, bottom, left and right. Once a margin is set in Microsoft Word, you cannot type in that area. Microsoft Word has default margins set at 1" on the left side of the paper, 1" on the right side of the paper, 1" on the bottom of the paper, and 1" on the top of the paper. You can see these margins in the ruler bars (illustrated in the following figure) located on the left side of the Microsoft Word screen and at the top of the Microsoft Word screen. The rulers measure the size of your paper and help you judge distances. The rulers also show you the area of your margins. The white area on a ruler bar displays your typing area. The blue area on the ruler bar shows your margins. In order to view your ruler bars, you must click on the small "ruler bar" button located just above Microsoft Word's scroll bar. To remove the ruler bars, click on the "ruler bar" button again.

Note: You can also display the rulers by opening the VIEW ribbon. In the SHOW/HIDE section, you will see the option RULER. To display the rulers, click in the checkbox in front of the option to put a checkmark in the box. To turn off the rulers, click in the checkbox to uncheck the box.

The "Ruler Bar" button.

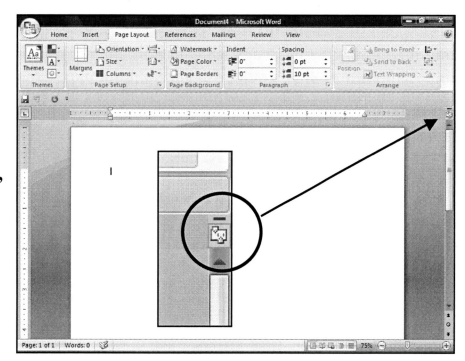

Chapter 14: Page Layout and Margins

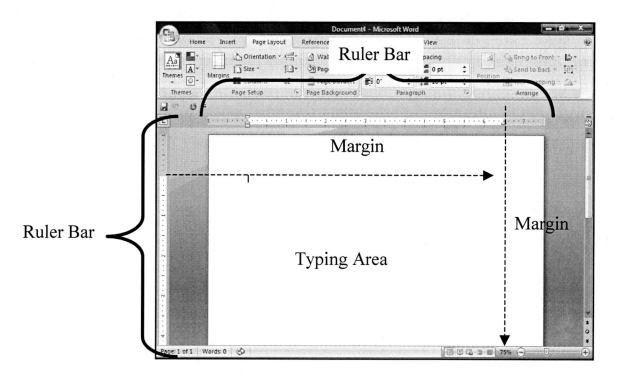

Microsoft Word automatically prevents accidental typing within the margins. When you first open a new blank document, look at the blinking cursor. It will *not* be blinking in the extreme upper left corner of the page. The blinking cursor will be placed exactly 1" from the top of the page and 1" from the left side of the page. As you type, as soon as your blinking cursor reaches the right margin, 1" from the right side of the page, Microsoft Word automatically moves your blinking cursor down one line and back to the left side of the page. When you reach the bottom margin of the page, Word automatically moves your blinking cursor to the next page.

Chapter 14: Page Layout and Margins

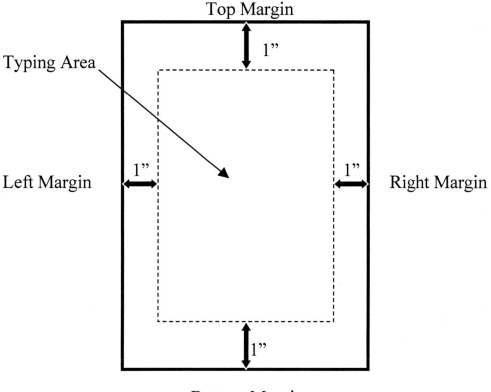

Top Margin

1"

Typing Area

Left Margin   1"   1"   Right Margin

1"

Bottom Margin

Page Size (Default = 8 ½" x 11")

Microsoft Word always starts with the standard 8 ½" x 11" page size. Since the majority of printer paper is sold in this standard size, users normally do not have to worry about setting or changing the paper size. You just type your letter and press the print option.

Text Size (Default = 12 pt.)

As discussed in section 6, you can change the text size. Microsoft Word always starts with size 12 point text, the standard text size used in business. Remember, the smaller the number, the smaller the text size.

Font Type (Default = Times New Roman)

As discussed in section 6, you can change the text style. Times New Roman, the standard font used in business, is the default setting in Microsoft Word.

Chapter 14: Page Layout and Margins

Text Alignment (Default = Left Alignment)

When you open a new blank document in Microsoft Word, look at the location of the blinking cursor. It's always placed in the upper left corner of the document. As you begin typing, the text will line up with the left margin of the page. This occurs because the default text alignment for Microsoft Word is set to Left Alignment.

Section 31: Changing Your Page Set-Up

Changing Page Margins (Default Settings)

Default settings make using Microsoft Word simple. As long as the default settings fit your needs, you just open Microsoft Word and start typing. However, you may want or need to change the layout of your page. One major feature of any document is the margin. Margins significantly affect how much information fits on a page. Increase your margins, and you will decrease the amount of space you have for your text. Decrease your margins, and you will increase the amount of space you have for your text.

Margins can be easily changed by using the MARGINS option located on the Page Layout ribbon. Click on the PAGE LAYOUT tab, and move your mouse arrow over the Page Setup section of the ribbon. Click once on the MARGINS option to display a list of pre-set margins. Move your mouse down the list, and click on the margin you would like to use. A successful click on any margin in the list will automatically apply that margin to your document. If you want to change your margin back to its original setting, click on the first option in the list labeled NORMAL.

Chapter 14: Page Layout and Margins

Changing Page Margins (Default Choice): Step by Step Instructions

1. Click the PAGE LAYOUT tab.
2. Click the MARGINS option.
3. Slide your arrow onto to the list of margin options.
4. Click on the margin of your choice.

Changing Page Margins (Default Settings): Visual Guide

Step 1:
Click the PAGE LAYOUT Tab.

Step 2:
Click the MARGINS option.

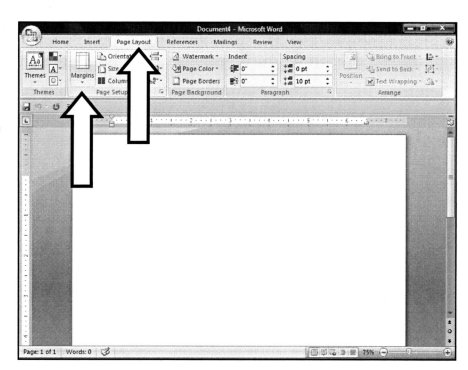

Chapter 14: Page Layout and Margins

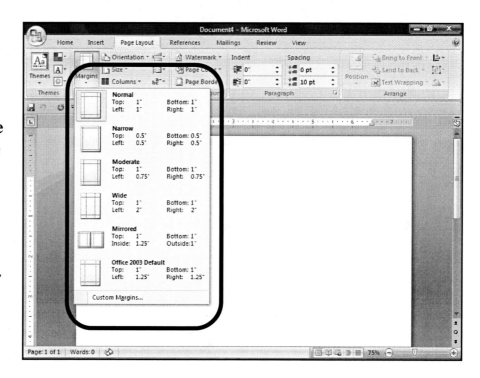

Step 3:
Slide the mouse arrow onto the list of margin options.

Step 4:
Click on the margin of your choice.

Changing Page Margins (Customized Settings)

If you would like to change the margin of your document to a measurement that is not available in the listed pre-set margins, click on the PAGE LAYOUT tab. Slide the mouse over the PAGE SETUP section of the Page Layout ribbon, and click once on the MARGINS option. The list of default margin options will be displayed. Located at the bottom of the margin options list is the option CUSTOM MARGINS. Click one time on the option CUSTOM MARGIN. The Page Setup Options screen will appear. The Page Setup Options screen has three tabs at the top: Margins, Paper, and Layout. Make sure the "Margins tab" has been selected by clicking once on the MARGINS tab. If you have successfully chosen it, you will see the heading "Margins" near the top of the Page Setup option screen.

Located just below the heading "Margins" are six input boxes containing the current margin settings. These six input boxes will be labeled: Top, Bottom, Inside, Outside, Gutter, and Gutter Position. Don't worry about Gutter and Gutter position which are only used for bound documents. It is highly unlikely you will ever need to use them. If you want to change any of your margins (Inside, Outside, Top, and Bottom) click once in the margin's input box. The number inside the margin's input box will turn blue. Press the Backspace key on the keyboard to erase the number, and type in the new desired margin. Be aware the margin cannot be set lower than 0.5." As you change your page margins, notice the preview screen located at the bottom of the Page Setup Options screen. The preview screen displays how your margin changes will affect your document.

NOTE: The Gutter option is used when typing a book that will eventually be printed and bound. Gutter refers to the area on a page that is designated to be cut off and lost during the book binding process. The gutter is always blank so no text is cut off during the binding process.

Located below the preview area is the heading APPLY TO. After you have changed your margins, make sure the input box just below the heading APPLY TO contains the option WHOLE DOCUMENT. If it does not say WHOLE DOCUMENT, you will end up having different margins on the other pages of your document. If the box does not contain WHOLE DOCUMENT, click on the drop down arrow next to it. A drop down list will open. Click on the option WHOLE DOCUMENT to select it. The input box will now contain the selection WHOLE DOCUMENT.

After you have changed your margins and want to apply your changes, click the OK button located at the bottom of the Page Setup options screen. If you do not want to keep your changes, click the CANCEL button. You will be returned to your document, and no changes will be made.

Changing Page Margins (Custom Settings): Step by Step Instructions

1. **Click the PAGE LAYOUT tab.**
2. **Click the MARGINS option.**
3. **Click CUSTOM MARGINS.**
4. **Click the MARGINS tab.**
5. **Click in the appropriate margin's input box and change the size of the margin.**
6. **Make certain "Apply to: Whole Document" has been selected.**
7. **Click the OK button**

Chapter 14: Page Layout and Margins

Changing Page Margins (Custom Settings): Visual Guide

Step 1:
Click the PAGE LAYOUT tab.

Step 2:
Click the MARGINS option.

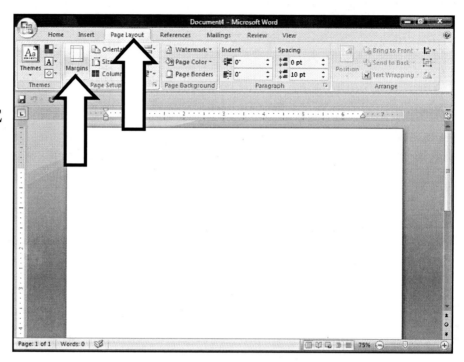

Step 3:
Click CUSTOM MARGINS.

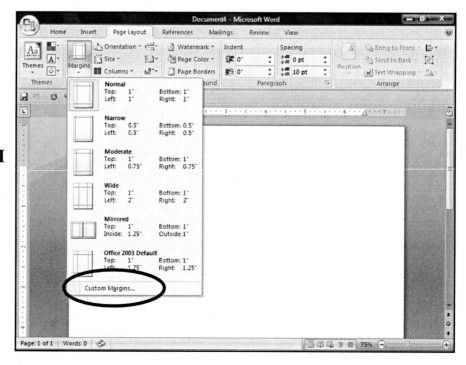

Chapter 14: Page Layout and Margins

Step 4:
Click the MARGINS tab.

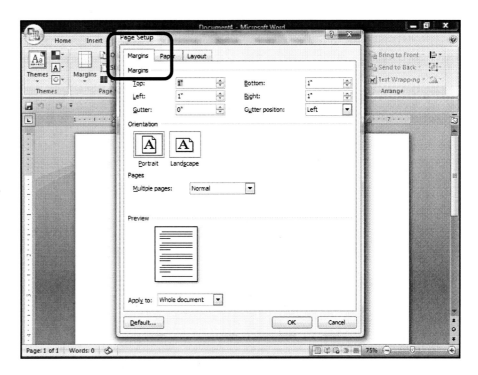

Step 5:
Click in the appropriate margin's input box and change the margin size.

Step 6:
Make sure APPLY TO: WHOLE DOCUMENT has been selected.

Step 7:
Click the OK button.

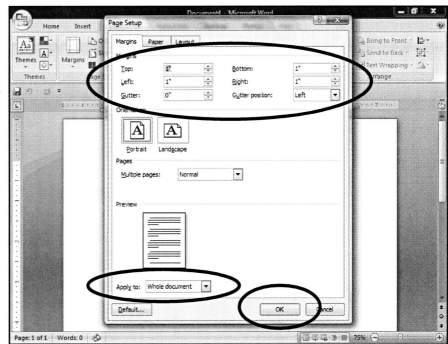

Chapter 14: Page Layout and Margins

Changing Page Orientation

The pages of your document can be set up vertically, called portrait, or horizontally, called landscape. Remember, Microsoft Word's default orientation is Portrait (vertical). If you want to change the orientation of your document, click the PAGE LAYOUT tab. Slide the mouse arrow over the PAGE SETUP section of the Page Layout ribbon, and click the ORIENTATION option. A small menu containing two choices will be displayed. Click LANDSCAPE. The orientation of your document will be changed.

RECOMMENDATION: Make all of your page setup decisions prior to starting the document so you can see how the text will lay out as you type your document. If you change the page set-up after the document has been written, the margins may dramatically affect the appearance of each page.

Changing Page Orientation: Step by Step Instructions
1. **Click the PAGE LAYOUT tab.**
2. **Click the ORIENTATION option.**
3. **Click either Portrait or Landscape.**

Changing Page Orientation: Visual Guide

**Step 1:
Click the PAGE
LAYOUT option.**

**Step 2:
Click the
ORIENTATION
option.**

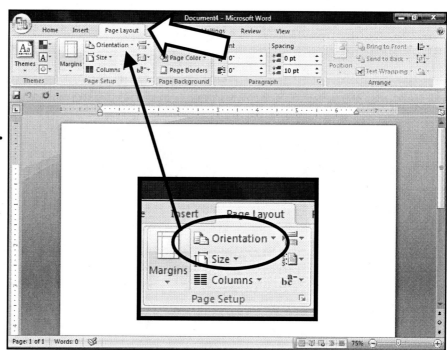

Step 3:
Click either
Portrait or
Landscape.

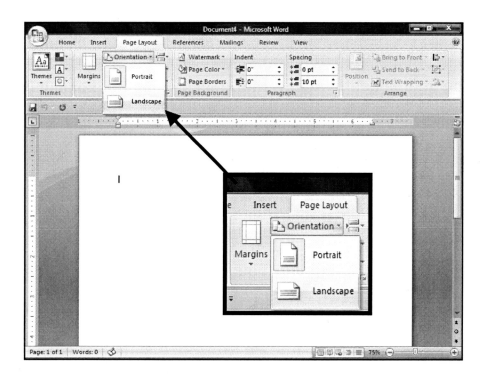

Chapter 14: Page Layout and Margins

<u>Chapter 15</u>

Working with Pictures

What You Will Learn in this Chapter
- ✓ Inserting a picture into a document
- ✓ Changing the size of a picture inserted into a document
- ✓ The term "text wrapping"
- ✓ Changing a picture's text wrapping
- ✓ Moving a picture within a document

Chapter 15: Working with Pictures

Section 32: Inserting Pictures into Documents

How to Add a Picture to a Document

Microsoft Word enables you to jazz up your documents by adding pictures. In the following examples, you will practice adding pictures to a document. The pictures you will use are pre-loaded on the computer in the PICTURES folder on your hard drive. The same steps you use to add pre-loaded pictures to your document can be used to add pictures which are stored elsewhere on your computer.

NOTE: Additional pictures can be found on the Internet, on CDs, or in files previously saved to the computer. Many people add additional pictures to their computer through e-mails, digital cameras, and scanners.

To practice adding pictures to a document, imagine you just came back from vacation and loaded all your vacation pictures onto your computer. You are going to create a document in Microsoft Word that will help capture your vacation's highlights.

To begin, open a new blank document. At the top of the page type the word VACATION. Move the blinking cursor down three of four lines by pressing the ENTER key on the keyboard. You are now ready to insert a picture below the title VACATION. To add a picture, click on the INSERT tab to display the Insert ribbon. Move your mouse arrow on top of the ILLUSTRATIONS section, and click on the option PICTURE. The "Insert Pictures screen" will appear, enabling you to look through the pictures stored on your computer. The computer is designed to begin looking in the last place you searched for an item. For example, if you inserted a picture stored in the Documents folder, the contents of the Documents folder will be displayed. If the last picture you inserted was located in the Pictures folder, the contents of the Pictures folder will be displayed, etc.

The pictures you are looking for are located in the Pictures folder. To view the contents of the Pictures folder, locate the title FAVORITE LINKS. Favorite Links will be located on the left side of the "Insert Pictures" screen. Located below the title Favorite Links is the option Pictures. Click one time on the option Pictures. The contents of the Pictures folder will be displayed in the large white area in the middle of the "Insert Pictures" screen.

NOTE: The large white area in the middle of the "Insert Pictures" screen displays the contents of the currently selected folder.

Located in the Pictures folder is a folder named Sample Pictures which contains several pictures. To see the contents of the Sample Pictures folder, double click it. After a successful double click, the contents of the Sample Pictures folder will be displayed in the large white area in the middle of the "Insert Pictures" screen.

The sample pictures folder contains fifteen pictures including titles such as Autumn Leaves, Waterfall, Tree, etc. Congratulations! You have found your pictures. Click once on the picture you want to insert. In this example, click on the picture HUMPBACK WHALE. An orange highlight will surround the picture. Click the INSERT button located in the lower right corner of the "Insert Pictures" screen. The picture will be inserted into your document where your blinking cursor had been placed.

In your document, your blinking cursor should be located just to the right of the picture of the Humpback Whale. Type the name of the picture, Humpback Whale, and press the Enter key on the keyboard two or three times to move the blinking cursor further down the page.

Chapter 15: Working with Pictures

Inserting Pictures: Step by Step Instructions
1. Type the Title of your document.
2. Press the Enter key twice.
3. Place the blinking cursor on the document where you would like to insert the picture.
4. Click the INSERT tab.
5. Click the PICTURE option.
6. Locate the picture on your computer using the "Insert Picture" screen.
7. Select the picture from the list by clicking on the picture.
   a. Click on the SAMPLES PICTURES folder.
   b. Click on the picture you want to select it.
8. Click the INSERT button.
   - Your picture will be inserted at the location where the cursor was positioned.

Inserting Pictures: Visual Guide

Step 1:
Type the title:
Vacation.

Step 2:
Press the ENTER
key two times.

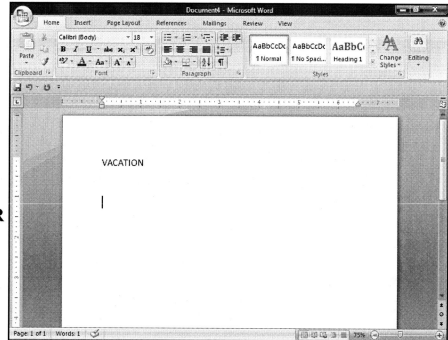

Chapter 15: Working with Pictures

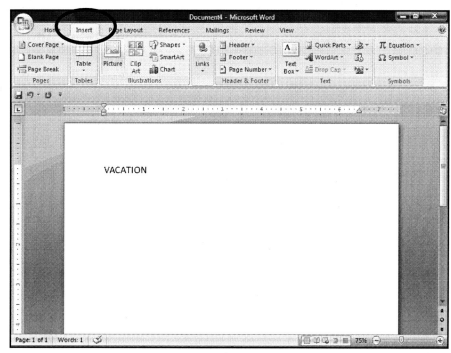

Step 3:
Place the cursor where you want to insert the picture.

Step 4:
Click the INSERT tab.

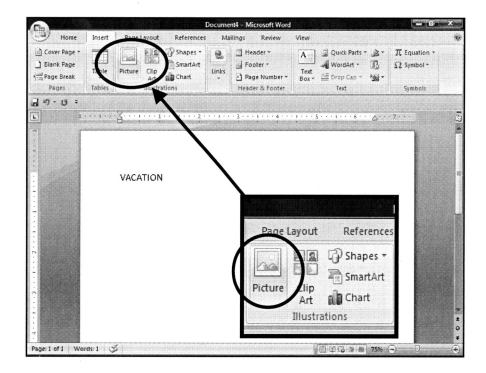

Step 5:
Click the PICTURE option.

**Step 6:
Locate the
picture using the
Insert Picture
screen.**

**Step 7:
Click
PICTURES.**

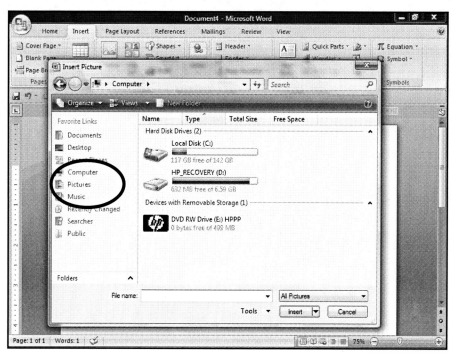

**Step 7a:
Click the
SAMPLE
PICTURES
folder.**

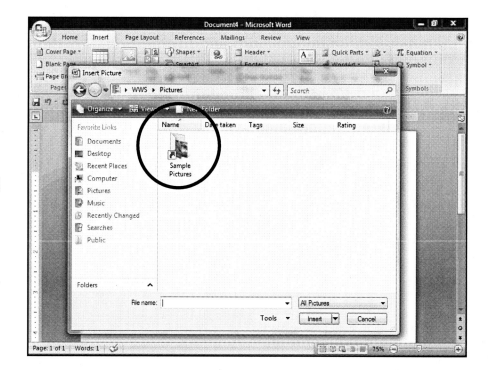

Chapter 15: Working with Pictures

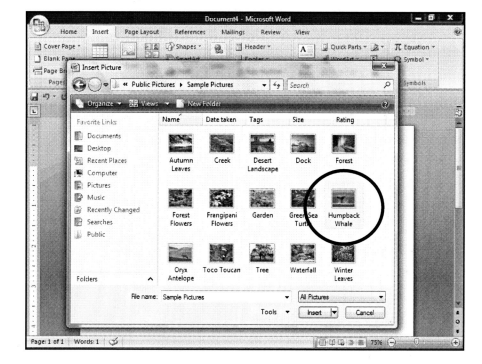

**Step 7b:
Click on the
picture:
Humpback
Whale.**

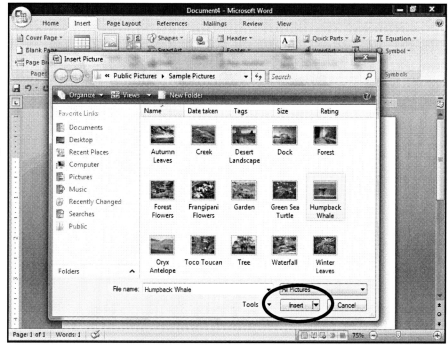

**Step 8: Click the
INSERT button.**

Chapter 15: Working with Pictures

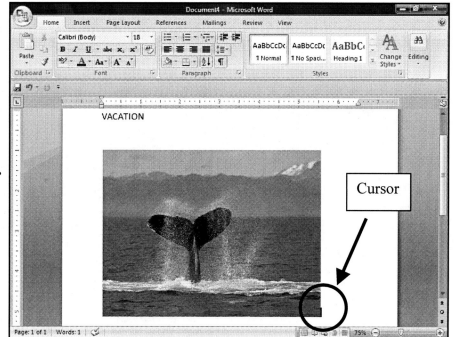

The picture is inserted where your blinking cursor is located.

Practice Inserting a Second Picture (The Forest)

Follow the same steps to insert the picture of the forest. Place the blinking cursor where you want the picture to be inserted. (The blinking cursor should still be located just after the picture of the humpback whale.) Press the Enter key on the keyboard twice to move the blinking cursor further down the page. Click the INSERT tab. Click the PICTURE option. The Insert Picture screen will appear.

Since you just inserted a picture located in the Sample Pictures folder, the contents of the Sample Picture folder will automatically be displayed on the Insert Picture screen. Click on the picture of the Forest and, finally, click on the INSERT button located in the lower right corner of the Insert Picture screen. The picture of the Forest will be added to your document.

Practice Inserting a Second Picture (The Forest): Step by Step Instructions

1. **Press the Enter key twice.**
2. **Click the INSERT tab.**
3. **Click the PICTURE option.**
4. **Click on a picture to select it.**
5. **Click the INSERT button.**

Chapter 15: Working with Pictures

Practice Inserting a Second Picture (The Forest): Visual Guide

Step 1:
Press the ENTER key on the keyboard twice.

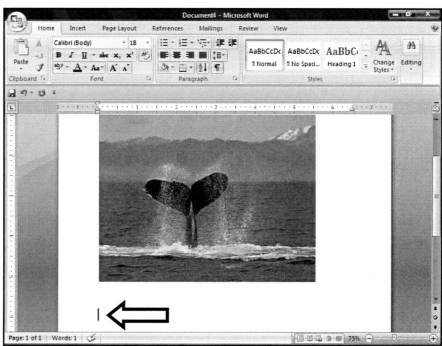

Step 2:
Click the INSERT tab.

Step 3:
Click the PICTURE option.

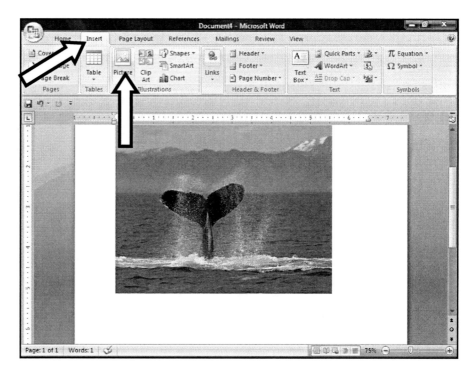

Chapter 15: Working with Pictures

Step 4:
Click on the picture of the Forest.

Step 5:
Click the INSERT button.

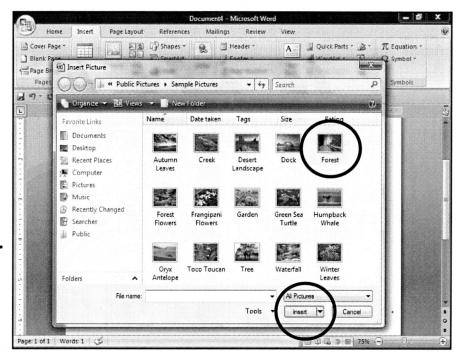

The picture has been added to your document.

Chapter 15: Working with Pictures

Section 33: Resizing Pictures

How to Change the Size of a Picture

Pictures come in all shapes and sizes. Some will be very large, others will be very small. Microsoft Word makes it easy to change the size of your picture. Click once on the picture you want to change to select it. After you click on it, a thin blue line will outline the picture and eight small blue squares/dots will appear around the edges. There will be one blue dot in each corner and one blue square in the middle of each side. These blue squares/dots are referred to as "crop dots."

"Crop dots" enable you to change the size of the picture. Place your mouse arrow on top of any of these "crop dots," and your mouse arrow will turn into a double arrow. While your mouse arrow looks like a double arrow, click *and hold down* the left mouse button.   While holding down the left mouse button, you can drag the sides of the picture up or down, left or right. To make your picture smaller, move the mouse in towards the picture; to make the picture larger, move the mouse out, away from the picture. When you release the left mouse button, the picture will resize itself to fit the area you created by dragging the "crop dots."

HINT: When changing the size of a picture, always click and drag the corner "crop dots." Using the corner "crop dots" enables you to keep the pictures correct height to width ratio. If you click and drag a "crop dot" located on the side of the picture, you will distort the picture by making the picture too wide or too tall.

Chapter 15: Working with Pictures

Resizing Pictures: Step by Step Instructions

1. Click on the picture one time.
   - A thin blue line will outline the picture and eight small blue squares/dots will appear around the edges of the picture.
2. Place your mouse arrow over one of the "crop dots."
3. Click and hold down the left mouse button.
4. While holding down the left mouse button, drag the sides of the picture up or down, left or right.
5. Release the left mouse button,
   - The picture will resize itself to fit the area created by dragging the "crop dots."

Resizing Pictures: Visual Guide

Step 1:
Click on the
picture one time.

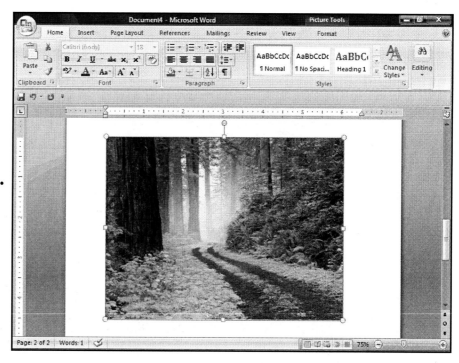

Step 2:
Place your mouse arrow over one of the "crop dots".

Step 3:
Click and hold down the left mouse button.

Step 4:
While holding down the left mouse button, drag the sides of the picture up or down, left or right.

**Step 5:
Release the left
mouse button.**

**The picture has
been resized.**

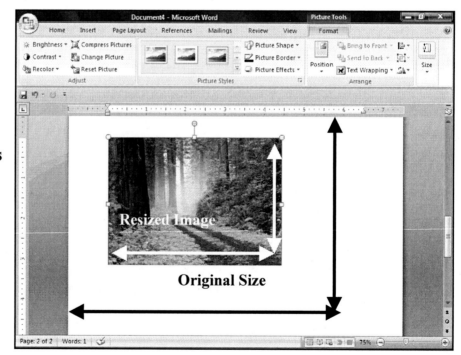

Chapter 15: Working with Pictures

Section 34: A Word about Wrapping Style

What is Wrapping Style?

An important aspect of working with pictures is being able to move pictures within the document. Before you begin moving pictures around a document, it is very important to understand the term WRAPPING STYLE which refers to "how the inserted picture will react with the surrounding text. Will the picture you add cover your text, lay behind the text, push the text out of the way, etc.? There are five basic types of wrapping styles -- Behind Text, In Front of Text, In Line with Text, Square, and Tight.

NOTE: The computer will randomly assign a wrapping style for each picture you insert. It is up to you to change the wrapping style so the picture appears how and where you want it.

Overview of Picture Wrapping Styles:

Behind Text: When you insert the picture, it will not affect the placement of the surrounding text. The picture will be placed behind any text in your document. You have the ability to type directly on top of the picture and move the picture anywhere on the page.

In Front of Text: When you insert the picture, it will not affect the placement of the surrounding text. The picture will simply be placed directly on top of any text in your document. You will not be able to see any text located behind the picture. You can move the picture anywhere on the page.

In Line with Text: When you insert the picture, it will have the same qualities as text. The picture will move surrounding text out of the way, just like words typed into a document move text. The picture will not cover over, or be covered over, by any text in your document. The same rules apply to moving text apply to moving pictures.

Square: When you insert the picture, it will be independent of anything else in the document. The picture will not cover over, or be covered over, by text. It will push surrounding text out of the way, but leave a small white border around the image. This border will ensure the text lines up to the straight edge surrounding the image. With the square layout, you can move the picture anywhere on the page.

Tight: When you insert the picture, it will be independent of anything else in the document. The picture will not cover over, or be covered over, by text. It will push surrounding text out of the way, but the text will conform to the edge of the image. The tight layout also allows you to move the picture anywhere on the page.

HINT: Before you attempt to move a picture around a document, it is very important to know a picture's selected layout.

Changing a Picture's Wrapping Style

Double click a picture to view its wrapping style. A ribbon titled FORMAT will be displayed. The Format ribbon contains many handy options that help you edit your pictures. To change a picture's wrapping style, move the mouse arrow onto the ARRANGE section of the Format ribbon, and click on the TEXT WRAPPING option. A list of the text wrapping options will be displayed. Slide your mouse arrow on the list of options, and click your mouse arrow one time on any option to select it. A successful click will automatically apply the chosen text wrapping to your selected picture.

Changing a Picture's Wrapping Style: Step by Step Instructions

1. **Double click the picture.**
   - **The FORMAT ribbon will be displayed.**
2. **Click the TEXT WRAPPING option.**
3. **Click, one time, on the appropriate wrapping style.**

Changing a Picture's Wrapping Style: Visual Guide

Step 1:
Double click on the picture.

The FORMAT ribbon will be displayed.

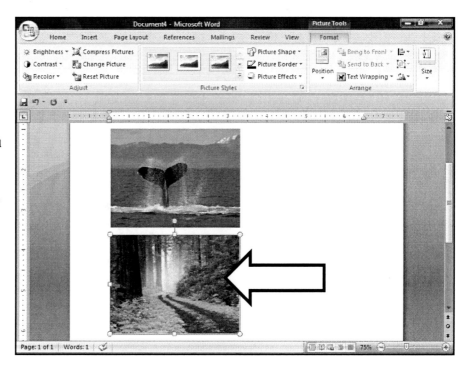

Step 2:
Click TEXT WRAPPING.

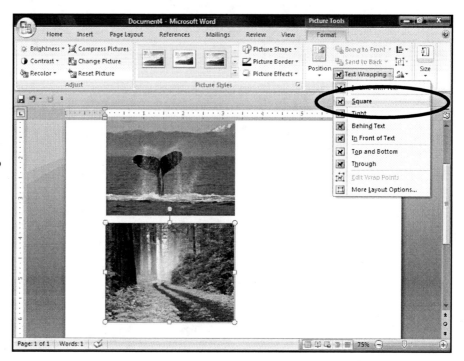

Step 3:
Click on the
desired layout.
In this example,
click SQUARE.

Section 35: Moving Pictures within a Document

How to Move a Picture

To move a picture, click on the picture once and hold down the left mouse button. Drag the picture to the desired location, and release the left mouse button to drop the picture into its new location. If the picture is not staying where you placed it, check/change its wrapping style and try again.

Chapter 15: Working with Pictures

Moving Pictures within a Document: Step by Step Instructions

1. Double click on the picture you want to move.
2. Click TEXT WRAPPING.
3. Click the desired layout.
4. Click on the picture and hold down the left mouse button.
5. While holding down the left mouse button, drag the picture to the desired location.
6. Release the left mouse button.

Moving Pictures within a Document: Visual Guide

Step 1:
Double click on the picture you want to move.

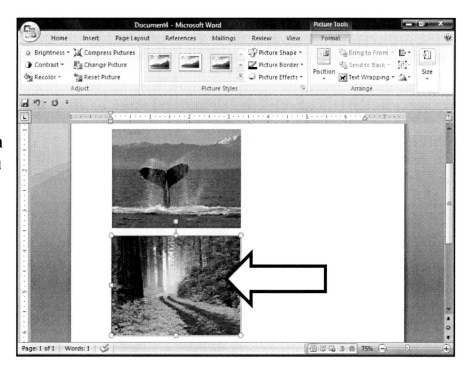

Chapter 15: Working with Pictures

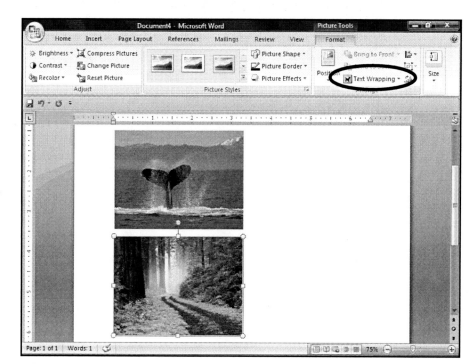

Step 2:
Click TEXT
WRAPPING.

Step 3:
Click on the
desired layout.
In this example,
click SQUARE.

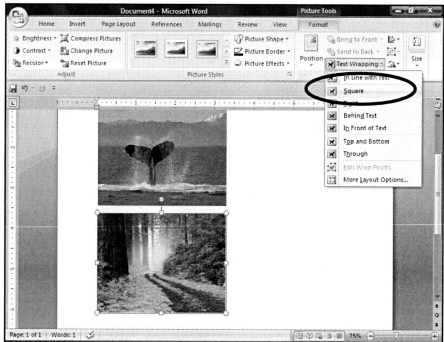

Step 4:
To move the picture, click on it and hold down the left mouse button.

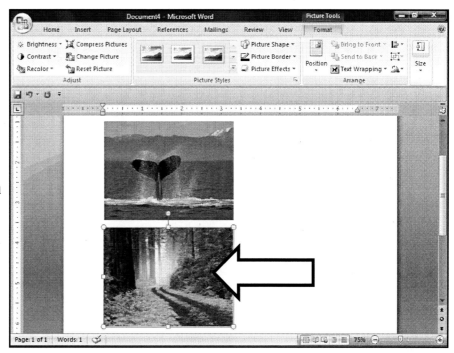

Step 5:
While holding the left mouse button down, drag the picture around the page.

Step 6:
Release the mouse button to drop the picture.

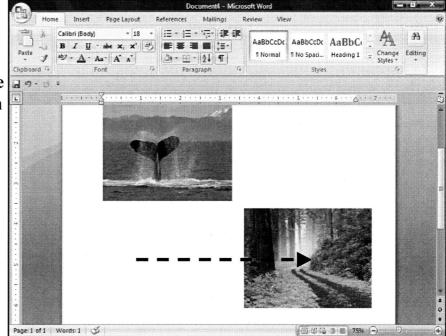

Chapter 15: Working with Pictures

Try it Again!

Step 4:
Click on the picture, and hold down the left mouse button

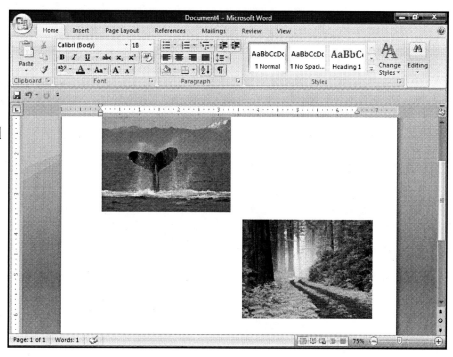

Step 5:
While holding the left mouse button down, drag the picture around the page.

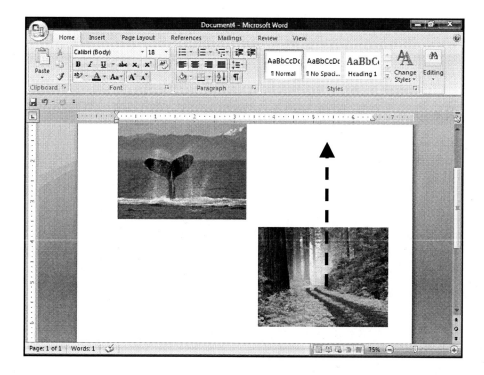

Step 6:
Let go of the left mouse button to drop the picture.

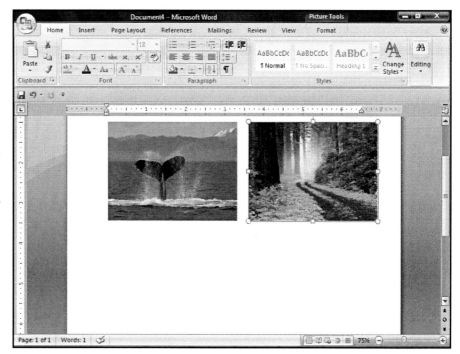

Chapter 15: Working with Pictures

Chapter 16

Columns

What You Will Learn in this Chapter
- ✓ Inserting columns into a document
- ✓ The term column break
- ✓ Inserting column breaks

Chapter 16: Columns

Section 36: Creating Columns Within a Document

The Columns Feature

Microsoft Word has a columns feature that enables users to separate lists into multiple vertical columns. Using the columns feature can add quite a bit of strength and organization to a document. Before separating your work into columns, we highly recommend that you type all of the text into your document first. This will prevent a great number of the complications that can arise when working with columns. We also suggest that you save your work prior to making the formatting changes. If you've saved your document and don't like the results of changing text into columns, you can return to the saved, unchanged, copy.

In the following example, you will be working with three columns and a title as shown below.

Title: Columns…Up Close and Personal
Column number 1: Colors: Red, Blue, Green, Yellow, Black
Column number 2: Cars: Lincoln, Ford, Chevy, Acura, Toyota
Column number 3: Names: Jim, Nancy, Bill, Emily, Mike, Steve, Ed, Michelle

To begin the example, open a new blank document. Type the above data straight down the page as shown in the following illustration.

Chapter 16: Columns

The Process of Creating Columns

After you have finished typing, highlight the text you want to separate into columns. Do not highlight the title "Columns…Up Close and Personal." After you have highlighted the list of items, click on the PAGE LAYOUT tab. Move the mouse arrow over the PAGE SETUP section of the Page Layout ribbon, and click on the option COLUMNS. A list of six different "column" options will be displayed -- One, Two, Three, Left, Right, and More Columns. The first three options, One, Two and Three, enable you to select the number of columns you want to separate your text into. Options Left and Right separate the highlighted text into two columns, but one column will be narrow and one column will be wide. The Left and Right options are useful to use when you want to have one column of short titles and one column of longer descriptions. The last option, More Columns, provides advanced options. In this example, you want to put your data into three separate columns, so click once on the option THREE.

After clicking on the option "Three," your page will be divided into three separate columns. You can tell your page has been divided into three columns by looking at the ruler bar located across the top of the page. Remember, the margins on a ruler bar are light blue and typing sections are white.

Chapter 16: Columns

Inserting Columns: Step by Step Instructions

1. Type everything you would like to put into the columns.
2. Highlight the desired text.
3. Click the PAGE LAYOUT tab.
4. Choose the COLUMNS option.
5. Click the picture of the desired number of columns.

Inserting Columns: Visual Guide

Remember, margins on a ruler bar blue and typing sections are white.

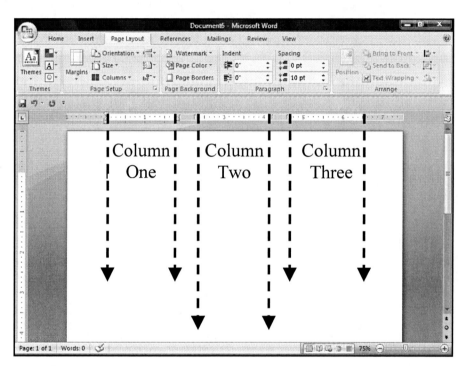

Chapter 16: Columns

Step 1:
Type your list.

Step 2:
Highlight the text that you want to separate into columns.

Chapter 16: Columns

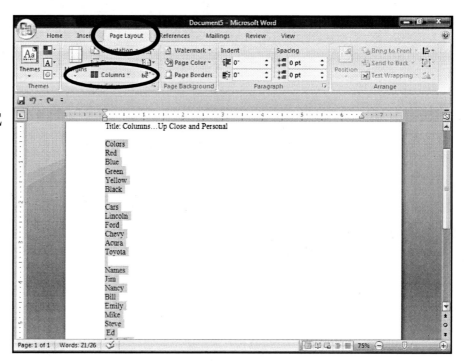

Step 3:
Click the PAGE LAYOUT tab.

Step 4:
Click the COLUMNS option.

Step 5:
Click the option: THREE.

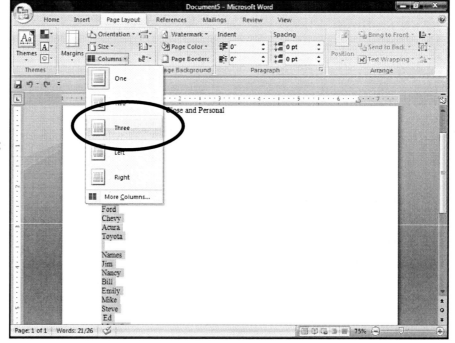

The text has been separated into three columns.

**Step 6:
Click anywhere on the page to unhighlight the text.**

Section 37: Column Breaks

Inserting Column Breaks

It is very common to separate your page into columns and end up having your text distributed unevenly or in the wrong columns. If this occurs, the best way to correct the problem is by inserting "column breaks." Column breaks tell the computer where you want the text in one column to end and the next column to begin. Column breaks should be inserted just in front of the item you want to move to the next column. Everything to the right of the column break will be moved to the next column.

To insert a column break, place your blinking cursor in front of the first item you want moved to the next column. Click the PAGE LAYOUT tab. Move the mouse arrow over the FONT section of the Page Layout ribbon, and click on the SECTION BREAK icon. A list of six different types of section breaks will be displayed. Move the mouse arrow over the options COLUMN, and click the left mouse button. The column break will be inserted.

HINT: The section break icon looks like two pieces of paper separated by a small gap.

In the following example, column breaks need to be inserted just before the "C" in cars and just before the "N" in names.

Chapter 16: Columns

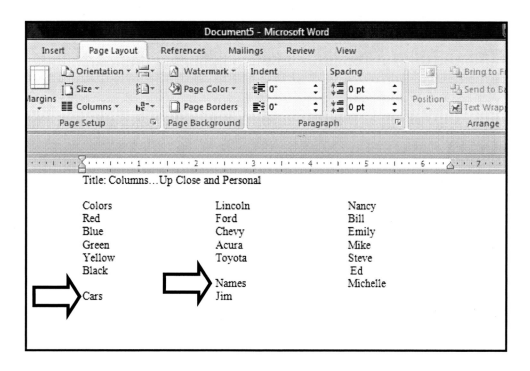

Inserting Column Breaks: Step by Step Instructions

1. Position the blinking cursor where you would like the next column to start.
2. Click the PAGE LAYOUT tab.
3. Click the SECTION BREAK icon.
4. Click the COLUMN option.

Chapter 16: Columns

Inserting Column Breaks: Visual Guide

Step 1:
Place your blinking cursor in front of the first item you want moved to the next column.

In this example, click before the letter "C" in Cars.

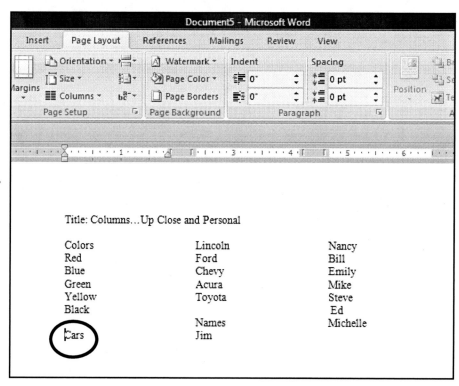

Step 2:
Click the PAGE LAYOUT tab.

Step 3:
Click the Section Break icon.

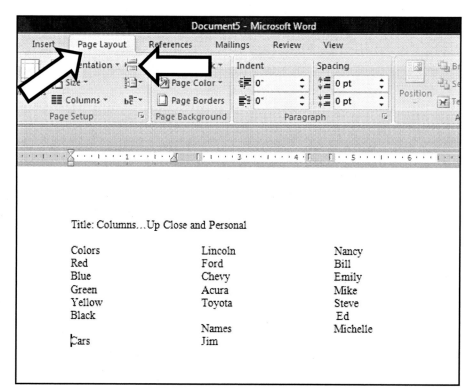

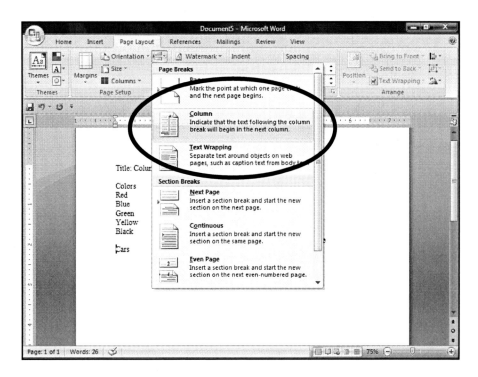

**Step 4:
Click the
COLUMN
option.**

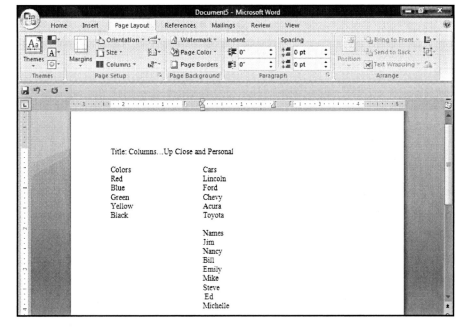

**The Column
Break has been
inserted.**

Chapter 16: Columns

Try it Again!

Step 1:
Place your blinking cursor in front of the first item you want moved to the next column.

In this example, click before the letter "N" in Names.

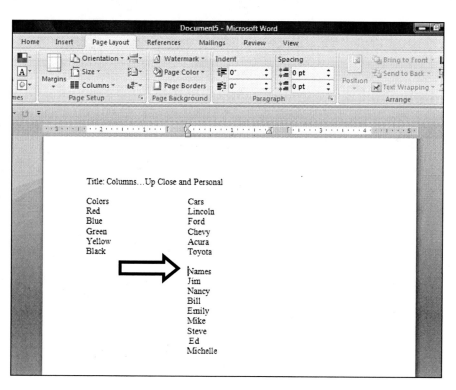

Step 2:
Click the PAGE LAYOUT tab.

Step 3:
Click the SECTION BREAK icon.

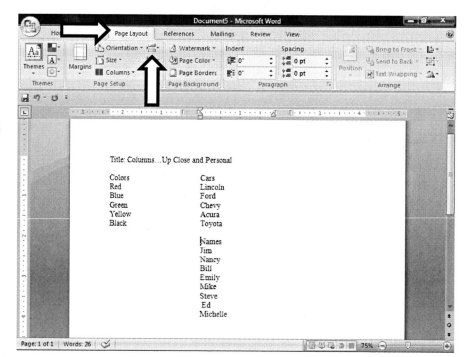

Chapter 16: Columns

**Step 4:
Click on the
COLUMN
option.**

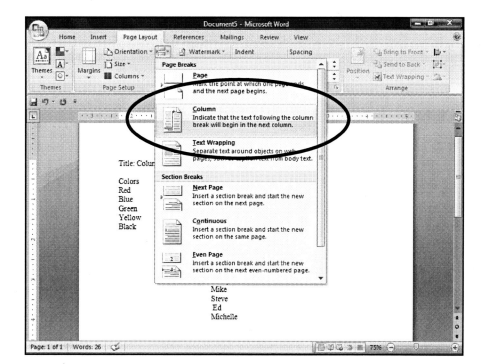

**The Column
Break has been
inserted.**

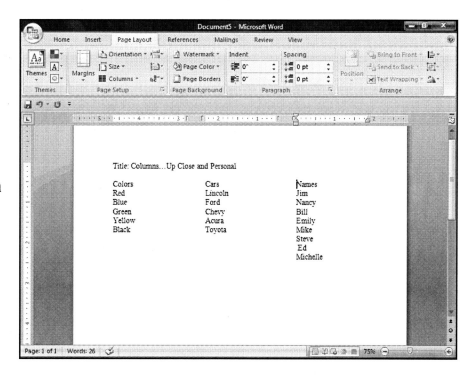

Chapter 16: Columns

For fun, add some finishing touches!

Capitalize, change the font size, bold, and center the Title.

Italicize, bold, and underline the Column Headings.

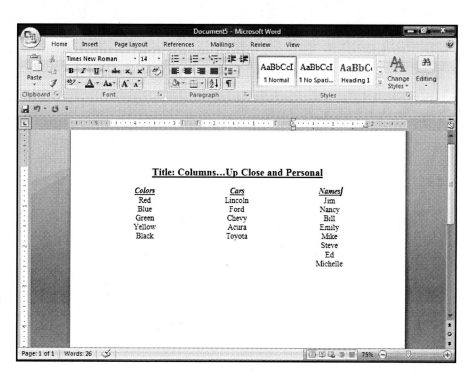

Chapter 17

Mail Merge

What You Will Learn in this Chapter
✓ The terms "Mail Merge" and "Field"
✓ Creating an address list
✓ Performing a successful mail merge

Chapter 17: Mail Merge

Section 38: Creating Your Address List

What is Mail Merge?

Mail merge is a feature of Microsoft Word that enables you to send a letter to multiple people without having to create a new custom document for each individual. In a business setting, mail merge works great for mailing out company newsletters. On a personal level, mail merge can save you quite a bit of time when sending holiday cards to all of your friends and relatives. To use the mail merge option, you need to type a list of names and addresses into the computer and save it. When you want to send a newsletter or holiday card, you can merge the list of names and addresses and print them on the newsletters, holiday card envelopes, or labels. Mail merge saves countless hours of handwriting each name and address individually on each newsletter or envelope. Sit back and relax; let the computer do the work.

Creating an Address List to Mail Merge

The first step in performing a mail merge is collecting the list of names and addresses. This list can be created in Microsoft Word, Excel, a database program like Access, or Outlook. To keep things simple, you will create the list using Microsoft Word. When you are creating the list of names and addresses, make certain to follow a strict format. If the format varies, even slightly, the mail merge will not work correctly.

The second step is choosing what format you will follow for each name. In this example, follow the following format: Name, Address, City, State, and Zip Code. Each piece of information is "technically" known as a field. For example, *Name* is a field, *Address* is a field, *City* is a field, etc. Each field should be separated by a comma.

Chapter 17: Mail Merge

NOTE: You can change the format you want to use. For example you could use the format: Name, Address, City, State, Country, County, and Zip OR Company, Name, Address, City, State, Zip. The important aspect to remember is that you have to use the same format for every person on your list.

Open Microsoft Word and type your list field names in the following format: Name, Address, City, State, and Zip. Remember to separate each field with a comma. Make sure you use the exact words, name, address, city, state, and zip, so that the computer can match your format style to the one it understands. After you finish typing your "field names," press the Enter key to move your blinking cursor down to the next line.

The next step is to type each individual's mailing information. Remember to separate each item with a comma, and press the Enter key at the end of each line when you start the next person.

In the following example, you will enter a small group of names and addresses. Later, you will learn how to add more names and addresses to the list.

Type the following information into Microsoft Word.

Name, Address, City, State, Zip
John Long, 27100 Chardon Rd, Chardon, Ohio, 44192
Amy Isabel, 115 Fairgrounds Ave, Willowick, Ohio, 55095
Richard Beric, 7103 Victoria Lane, Louisville, KY, 99089

After you have typed the above information, save this document to your computer and name it "address list." By saving the list, you insure that it will be available for future use. People often create several mailing lists and save each one separately on the computer. They may create one list containing the addresses of Christmas card recipients. Another list may contain the addresses of people to whom they send a family newsletter. Another list may contain the addresses of all the people they invite each year to Thanksgiving dinner, etc.

Once the list of addresses has been saved, close the Address List document.

Chapter 17: Mail Merge

Creating an Address List: Step by Step Instructions

1. Type the field names in the following format: Name, Address, City, State, Zip
2. Press the Enter key on the keyboard.
3. Type the addresses into Microsoft Word using the following format: Name, Address, City, State, Zip.
   - Press the Enter key, on the keyboard, after each address.
4. Click the OFFICE button.
5. Click the SAVE option.
6. Click the DOCUMENTS link.
7. Name the document "Address List."
8. Click the SAVE button.
9. Close the Address List document.

Creating an Address List: Visual Guide

Open Microsoft Word.

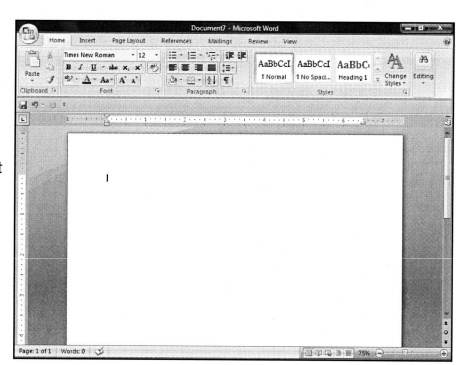

258

Chapter 17: Mail Merge

Step 1:
Type your field names in the correct format.

Step 2:
Press the Enter key.

Step 3:
Type the addresses, pressing the Enter key after each address.

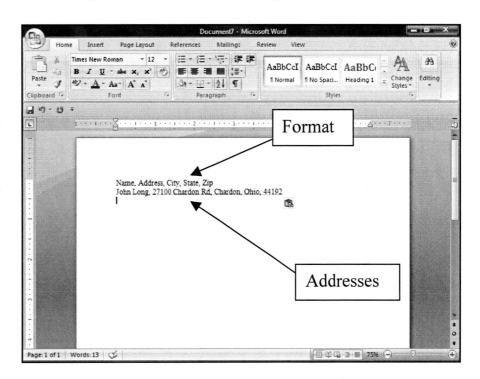

Remember to separate each field with a comma and to press the Enter key at the end of each line.

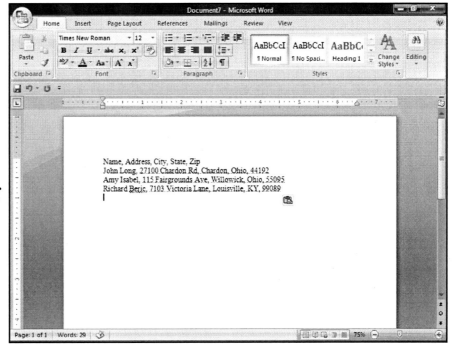

Save your work.

Step 4:
Click the
OFFICE Button.

Step 5:
Click the SAVE
option.

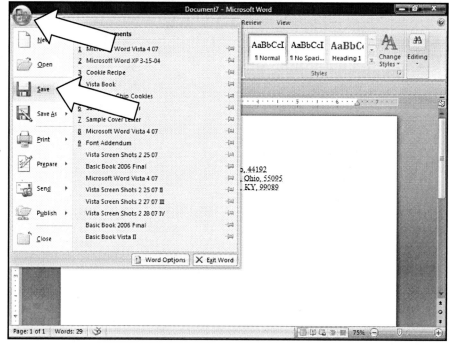

Save to
DOCUMENTS

Step 6:
Click the
DOCUMENTS
link.

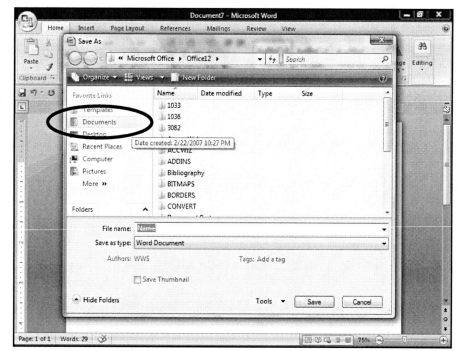

Step 7:
Name the
document
"Address List."

Step 8:
Click the SAVE
button.

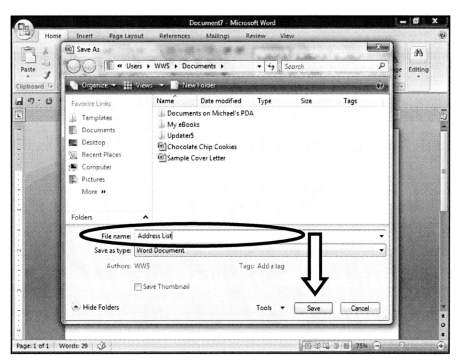

Step 9:
Close the
document.

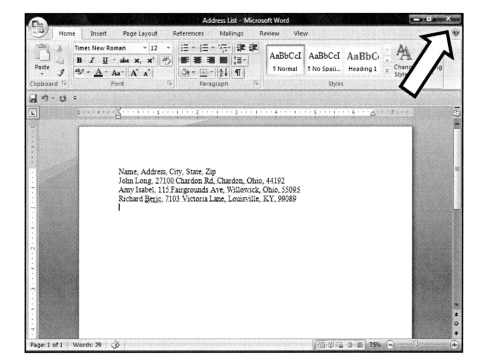

Chapter 17: Mail Merge

Section 39: Creating Your Mailing Labels

Using Your Address List to Create Mailing Labels

To perform a mail merge you must open a new, blank document. You will use this blank document to merge the list of addresses with mailing labels. To perform a mail merge, click on the MAILINGS tab to display the Mailings ribbon. Place your mouse arrow on top of the section START MAIL MERGE, and click on the START MAIL MERGE icon. A list of seven options will be displayed. Click on the option STEP BY STEP MAIL MERGE WIZARD. The wizard will display on the right side of the screen.

Located at the top of the Mail Merge Wizard screen is the heading "Select Document Type." Below this heading are five options -- Letter, E-Mail Message, Envelopes, Labels, and Directory. Click on the option LABELS. A successful click will place a small black dot in the circle next to the option labels.

Located at the bottom of the Mail Merge Wizard's screen will be the blue words NEXT: STARTING DOCUMENT. Click on them. The wizard will ask you how you want to set up your mailing labels. Halfway down the Mail Merge Wizard screen are the blue words LABEL OPTIONS. Click on Label Options to display the Label Options screen, which enables you to tell the computer what type and size of mailing labels you will use. This is an important step because the computer must know if your mailing labels are 1" x 2" or 2" x 4" or 1.5" x 3.5", etc. or it cannot print your labels correctly.

Most mailing labels purchased in stores have the company name and numeric codes written on the package. This data is also listed in Microsoft Word's memory. Your job is to match the name and label number found on your label package with the same information on the Label Options screen. The labels used in this example are Avery 5160.

The Label Options screen has two important sections. The first section is titled Label Vendors. To the right of this heading is a drop down box containing a list of label brands. Since Avery labels are being used in this example, click on the drop down arrow and select "Avery US Letter" from the list.

The second section of the Label options screen is titled Product Number. Located below this heading is a list of different labels and their numeric codes. Use the attached scroll bar, find the code 5160, and click on it. It will become highlighted. You have just told the computer that you are using Avery 5160 labels. Click the OK button. You will be returned to the Mail Merge wizard.

Click on NEXT: SELECT RECIEPIENTS located at the bottom of the Mail Merge screen. The wizard's next question is how you are going to provide the names and addresses for the labels you just selected. There are three options listed at the top of the wizard -- Use an Existing List, Select from Outlook Contacts, and Type a New List. Since you are going to use the Address List you just saved to your computer, select USE AN EXISTING LIST. It should have a black dot in the small circle on its left. If it does not have a black dot next to it, click in the small white circle and a black dot will appear.

The next step is to find the Address List you saved to the computer. Located in the middle of the Mail Merge Wizard screen will be the blue word BROWSE. Click on the word Browse to display the "Browse" screen, which enables you to look through your computer for the file *Address List*. This Browse screen has very similar properties to the Save Screen you used earlier to save the Address List to the Documents folder.

Located on the left side of the Browse screen will be the heading FAVORITE LINKS. Below this title is a list of locations on the computer. In this example, you saved the Address List to the Documents folder. Click on the word DOCUMENTS to display the contents of the Documents folder on the Browse screen. If you successfully saved the Address List to the Documents folder, the document "Address List" will now be displayed in the large white area in the center of the Browse screen. Click once on Address List. It will turn blue. Click on the OPEN button located on the right side of the Browse screen.

After you click the Open button, a new screen titled MAIL MERGE RECIPIENTS will appear, displaying a list of your addresses. This screen enables you to remove specific addresses from the list. To remove an address, simply click on the check box located directly to the left of the address. A successful click will remove the checkmark from the box, signifying that the address has been removed from the list. This address will still be saved in the address list document. It just won't be printed. To re-add the address, click on the empty check box again. A checkmark will reappear within the box. After you have completed adding and/or removing addresses, click the OK button.

WARNING: If your Address List contains an error, the MAIL MERGE RECIPIENTS list will not appear. It will be replaced by another screen titled HEADING DELIMINATORS. If the Heading Deliminators screen appears, close everything. Re-open your Address List and double check its formatting. You have forgotten to insert a needed comma, inserted too many commas, forgotten to press the Enter key after a line, or made another similar error while typing your addresses. After you have fixed the error(s), restart the mail merge process.

Your labels will display the words Next Record, indicating it will make a label for each person in the list. Click on the link NEXT: ARRANGE YOUR LABELS located at the bottom of the Mail Merge Screen. The wizard's wants to know what you want printed on the labels. There are five options: Address Block, Greeting Line, Electronic Postage, Postal Bar Code, and More Items. You want to put in the address information, so click on the link ADDRESS BLOCK. The Address Block Options screen will appear. Look at the white preview box to make sure the addresses are displayed correctly. Click the OK button located at the bottom right corner of the Address Block screen.

Look at the Mail Merge Screen located on the right side of your screen and click on the button labeled UPDATE ALL LABELS. If you do not see this button, it means there is more information located off the screen. Look for a small black arrow pointing down, located at the very bottom of the Mail Merge Screen, and place your mouse arrow on top of it. The Mail Merge Screen will scroll down, displaying more information, and the button will appear. After clicking on the UPDATE ALL LABELS button, your labels will be updated with the term Address Block.

Click on NEXT: PREVIEW YOUR LABELS located at the bottom of the Mail Merge screen, and your labels will be displayed with the addresses from the address list. If everything is correct, click NEXT: COMPLETE THE

Chapter 17: Mail Merge

MERGE located at the bottom of the Mail Merge screen. You will move to the next screen. Click on the print button to send the job to the printer. Remember to put the labels in the printer.

NOTE: Highlight all of the labels and choose center alignment to make sure that the words are in the middle of the labels and not too close to the edges.

Creating Mailing Labels: Step by Step Instructions

1. **Open a new blank Microsoft Word document.**
2. **Click the MAILINGS tab.**
3. **Click the START MAIL MERGE option.**
4. **Click the STEP BY STEP MAIL MERGE WIZARD option.**
5. **Click the LABELS option.**
6. **Click NEXT: STARTING DOCUMENT.**
7. **Click the LABEL OPTIONS button.**
8. **Click on the brand of labels you want from the Label Vendors list.**
9. **Click on your label's numeric code located in Product Numbers list.**
10. **Click the OK button.**
11. **Click NEXT: SELECT RECIPIENTS.**
12. **Click BROWSE.**
13. **Use the Browse screen to locate your Address List file.**
14. **Click on your Address List file.**
    - **The file will highlight in blue.**
15. **Click the OPEN button.**
    - **The Mail Merge recipients list will appear.**
16. **Remove any unwanted addresses at this time.**
17. **Click the OK button.**
18. **Click the NEXT: ARRANGE YOUR LABELS link located at the bottom of the Mail Merge Screen.**
19. **Click the ADDRESS BLOCK link.**
20. **Check to make certain the addresses are displayed correctly.**
21. **Click the OK button located in the bottom right corner of the Address Block screen.**

22. Click the UPDATE ALL LABELS link.
23. Click the NEXT: PREVIEW YOUR LABELS link.
24. Click the LAYOUT tab.
25. Click the SELECT option.
26. Click the SELECT TABLE option.
27. Click the Alignment button you want to use (Centered).
28. Click anywhere on the labels to un-highlight.
29. Click the NEXT: COMPLETE THE MERGE link.
30. Click the PRINT link.
31. Click in the circle to the left of ALL under Print records.
32. Click the OK button.
    - The final print screen will appear.
33. Click the OK button.

Creating Mailing Labels: Visual Guide

Step 1:
Open a new blank document.

Step 2:
Click the MAILINGS tab.

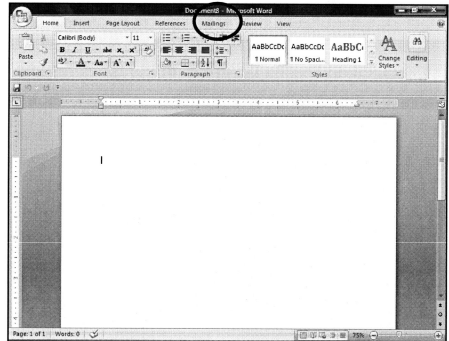

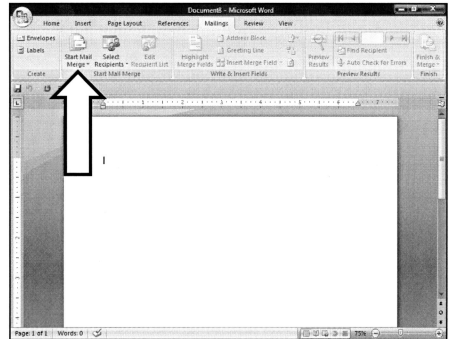

**Step 3:
Click START
MAIL MERGE.**

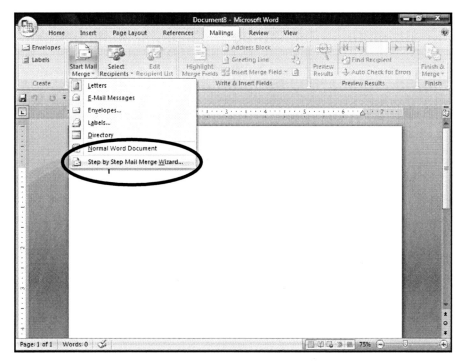

**Step 4:
Click the STEP
BY STEP MAIL
MERGE
WIZARD option.**

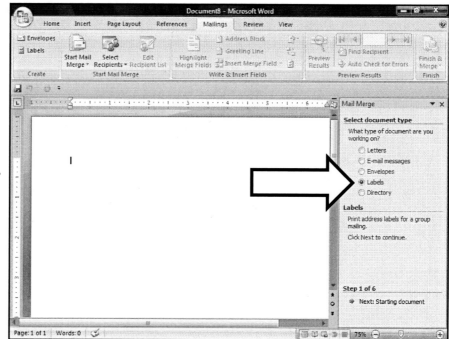

**Step 5:
Click the
LABELS option.**

**Step 6:
Click the
NEXT:
STARTING
DOCUMENT
link.**

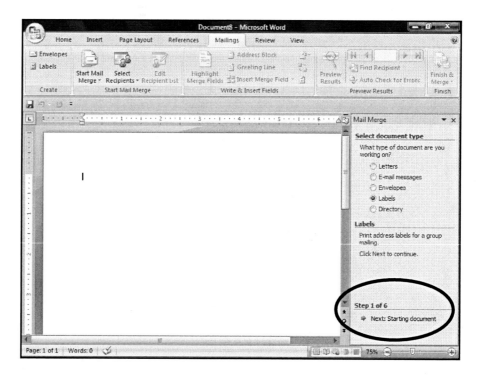

Chapter 17: Mail Merge

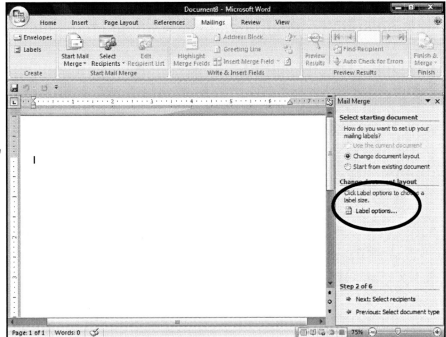

Step 7:
Click the LABEL
OPTIONS link.

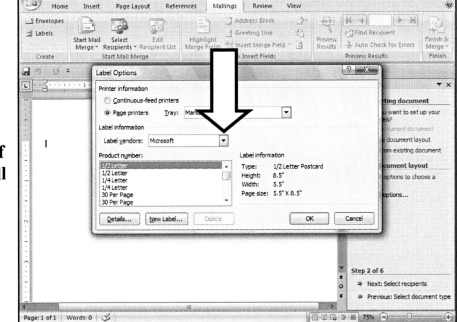

Step 8:
Select the
vendor's name of
the labels you will
be using.

Chapter 17: Mail Merge

Step 9:
Click on your label's numeric code located in the list of Product Numbers

Step 10:
Click the OK button

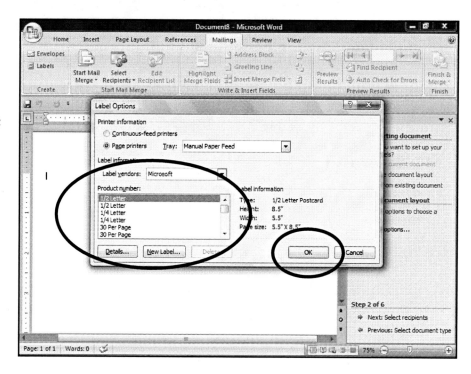

Step 11:
Click the NEXT: SELECT RECIPIENTS link.

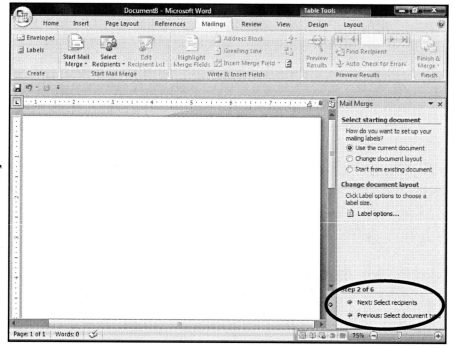

**Step 12:
Click the
BROWSE option.**

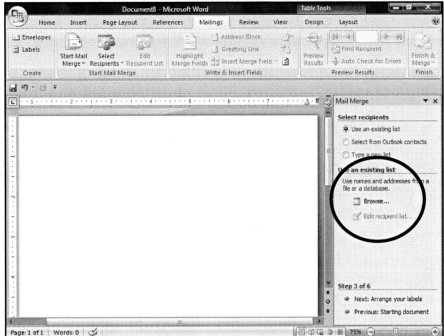

**Step 13:
Use the Browse
screen to locate
your Address
List.**

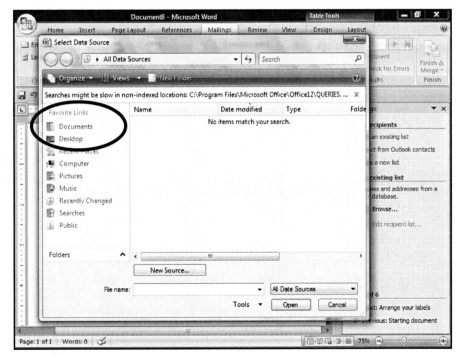

Step 14:
Click on your
file: *Address List.*

The file will
highlight in blue.

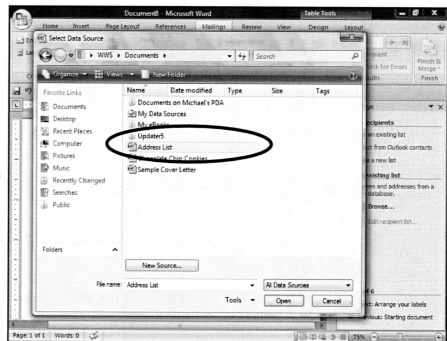

Step 15:
Click the OPEN
button.

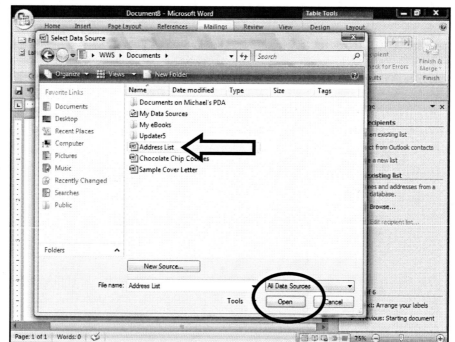

Step 16: Remove any unwanted addresses at this time by unchecking it.

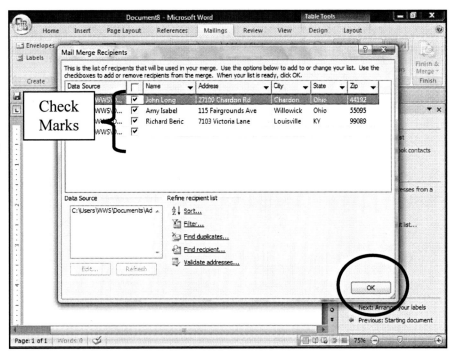

Step 17: Click the OK button.

Step 18: Click the NEXT: ARRANGE YOUR LABELS link.

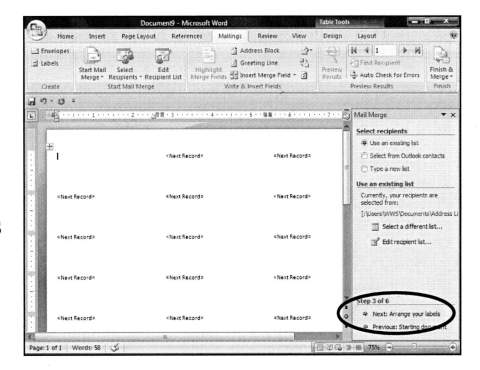

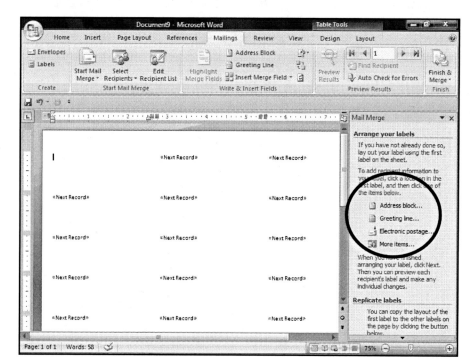

**Step 19:
Click the
ADDRESS
BLOCK link.**

**Step 20:
Check to make
sure the
addresses are
displayed
correctly.**

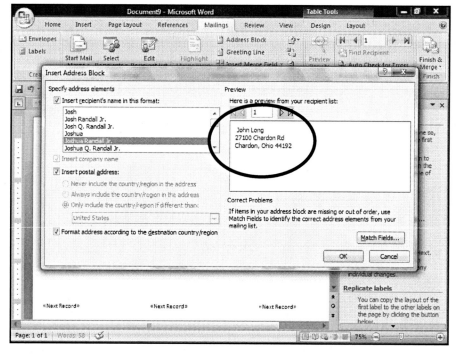

Chapter 17: Mail Merge

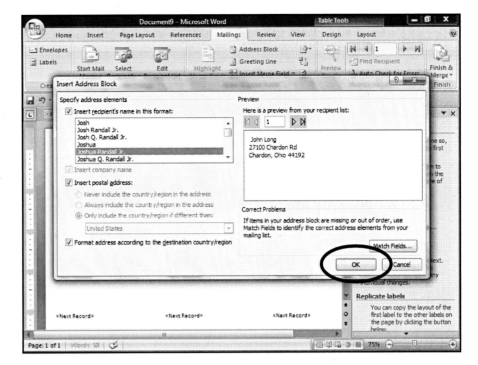

**Step 21:
Click the OK
button**

**Step 22:
Click the
UPDATE ALL
LABELS link.**

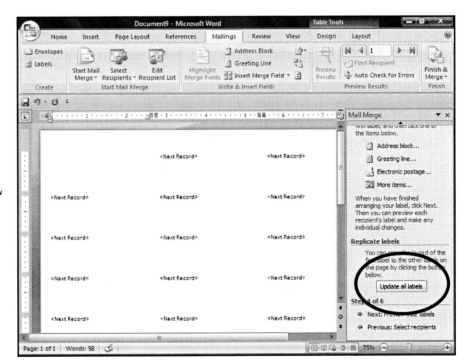

**Step 23:
Click the NEXT:
PREVIEW
YOUR LABELS
link.**

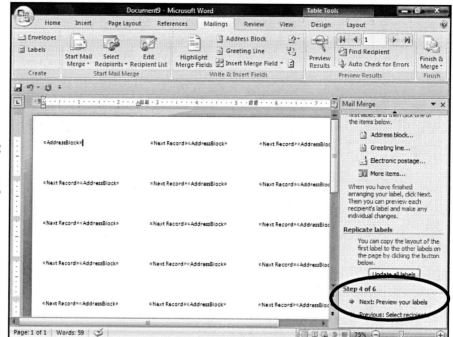

**The addresses
will be
individually
displayed in the
labels.**

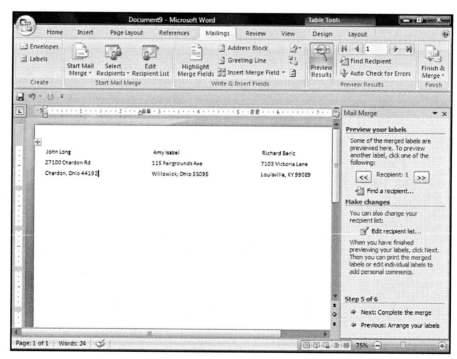

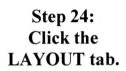

Step 24:
Click the
LAYOUT tab.

Step 25:
Click the
SELECT
option.

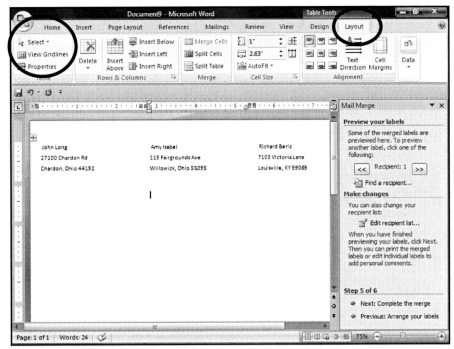

Step 26:
Click SELECT
TABLE.

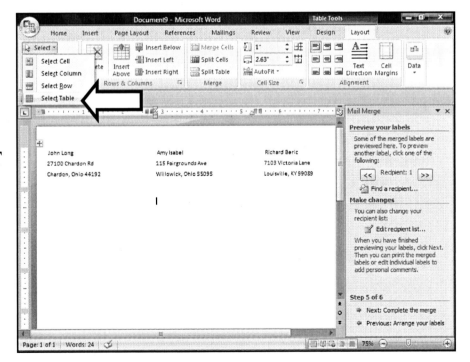

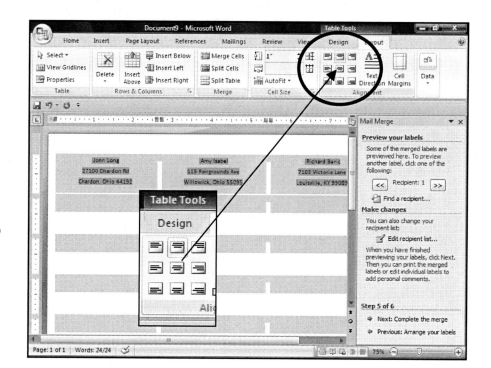

**Step 27:
Choose the
option
CENTERED**

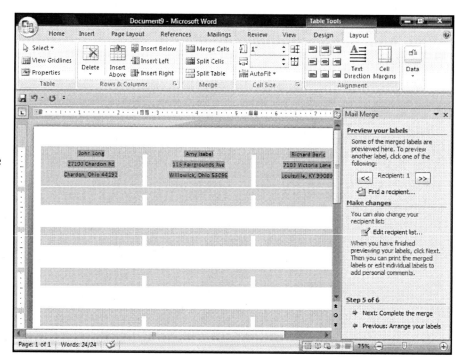

**Step 28:
Click anywhere
on the labels to
un-highlight.**

**Step 29:
Click the NEXT:
COMPLETE
THE MERGE
link.**

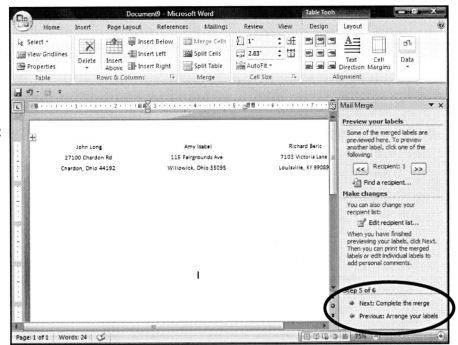

**Step 30:
Click the
PRINT link.**

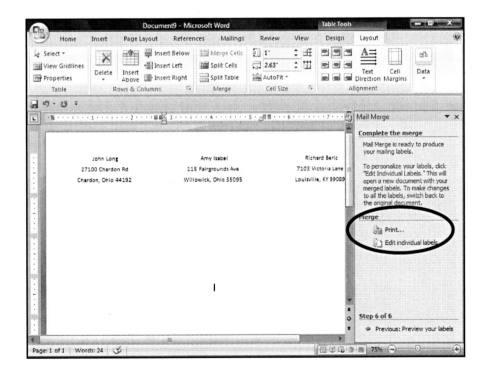

Step 31:
To print all the labels, choose ALL. Choose CURRENT RECORD to print one label. Choose FROM/TO to print selected labels.

Step 32:
Click the OK button.

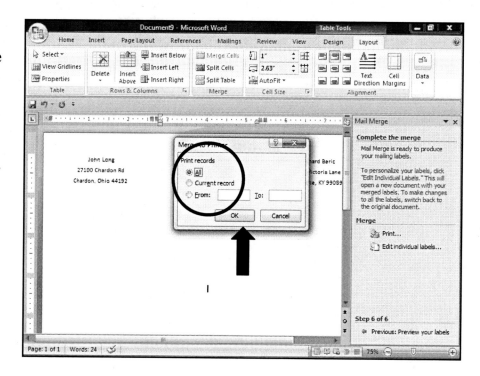

Step 33:
Click the OK button.

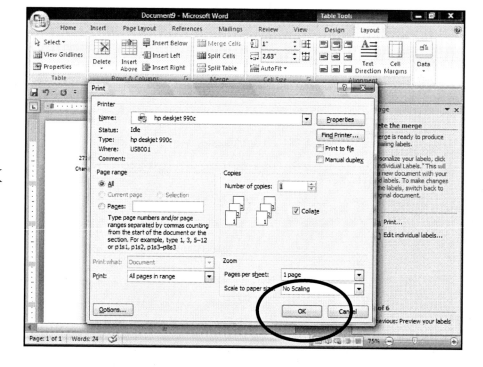

Chapter 17: Mail Merge

Click the X in the upper right corner of the screen and Microsoft Word will close. We hope you enjoyed the material found in this book as much as we enjoyed writing it for you. Please take time to review and keep on computing!

Congratulations! You have finished the course!

Index

Index

Appendix

Thank you for using the Web Wise Seniors' Basic Word Processing Computer book. We hope you enjoyed learning with it. Please let us know what you think of the book. If you found it easy to use and enjoyed the learning experience, please tell your family and friends.

Feel free to send your comments and feedback
to us at the following address:

Web Wise Seniors, Inc.
305 Woodstock Rd.
Eastlake, Ohio 44095

Or E-mail us at
WWS@WebWiseSeniors.com

Thank You!

Appendix

Web Wise Seniors is Proud to Present...
The "for Beginners" Series

	Title	Subtitle	ISBN #
Book	Basic Computers for Beginners	Windows XP	1-933404-45-0
Book	Basic Computers for Beginners	Windows Vista	1-933404-46-9
Book	Basic Internet for Beginners	Internet Explorer 7	1-933404-47-7
Book	Basic Email for Beginners		1-933404-48-5
Book	Microsoft Word 2007 for Beginners	Microsoft Word 2007	1-933404-49-3
Book	Microsoft Excel 2007 for Beginners	Microsoft Excel 2007	1-933404-50-7
Book	Microsoft Word for Beginners	Microsoft Word 2003	1-933404-51-5
Book	Microsoft Excel for Beginners	Microsoft Word 2003	1-933404-52-3
Large Print Books are $34.95 each.			

To Order Call Toll Free: 1-866-232-7032

	Title	Subtitle	ISBN #
Windows Vista Series			
DVD	Basic Computers Part 1 VISTA	Introduction for Beginners	1-933404-54-X
DVD	Basic Computers Part 2 VISTA	Essentials of the Keyboard	1-933404-55-8
DVD	Basic Computers Part 3 VISTA	Filing Fundamentals	1-933404-56-6
DVD	Basic Computers Part 4 VISTA	Customizing Your Computer	1-933404-57-4
DVD	The Internet Part 1 IE7	Searching the Internet	1-933404-58-2
DVD	The Internet Part 2 IE7	Better Searching Techniques	1-933404-59-0
DVD	E-mail Part 1 Windows Mail	The Basics	1-933404-60-4
DVD	E-mail Part 1 Windows Mail	Advanced Techniques	1-933404-61-2
Windows XP Series			
DVD	Basic Computers Part 1 XP	Introduction for Beginners	1-933404-74-4
DVD	Basic Computers Part 2 XP	Essentials of the Keyboard	1-933404-75-2
DVD	Basic Computers Part 3 XP	Filing Fundamentals	1-933404-76-0
DVD	Basic Computers Part 4 XP	Customizing Your Computer	1-933404-77-9
DVD	The Internet Part 1 IE6	Searching the Internet	1-933404-78-7
DVD	The Internet Part 2 IE6	Better Searching Techniques	1-933404-79-5
DVD	E-mail Part 1 Outlook Express	The Basics	1-933404-80-9
DVD	E-mail Part 2 Outlook Express	Advanced Techniques	1-933404-81-7

Additional Titles on the Next Page

Appendix

Web Wise Seniors is Proud to Present...
The "for Beginners" Series

	Title	Subtitle	ISBN #
Microsoft Office 2007 Series			
DVD	Word 2007 Part 1	An Introduction to Word Processing	1-933404-62-0
DVD	Word 2007 Part 2	Essential Word Tools	1-933404-63-9
DVD	Excel 2007 Part 1	An Introduction to Spreadsheets	1-933404-64-7
DVD	Excel 2007 Part 2	Essential Tools	1-933404-65-5
Microsoft Office 2003 Series			
DVD	Word Part 1	An Introduction to Word Processing	1-933404-82-5
DVD	Word Part 2	Essential Word Tools	1-933404-83-3
DVD	Word Part 3	Bullets and Numbers	1-933404-84-1
DVD	Word Part 4	Mail Merge and More	1-933404-85-X
DVD	Excel Part 1	An Introduction to Spreadsheets	1-933404-86-8
DVD	Excel Part 2	Essential Tools	1-933404-87-6
DVD	PowerPoint Part 1	Creating a Presentation	1-933404-88-4
DVD	PowerPoint Part 2	Transitions and More	1-933404-89-2
DVD	Publisher Part 1	An Introduction to Publisher	1-933404-90-6
DVD	Publisher Part 2	Utilize the Power of Publisher	1-933404-91-4
DVD	Outlook Part 1	An Introduction to Outlook	1-933404-92-2
DVD	Outlook Part 2	The Tools of Outlook	1-933404-93-0
Spanish DVD Series			
DVD	Basic Computers XP Part 1	Introduction for Beginners	1-933404-67-1
DVD	Basic Computers Vista Part 1	Introduction for Beginners	1-933404-66-3
DVD	Basic Computers Vista Part 2	Essentials of the Keyboard	1-933404-70-1
DVD	Basic Computers Vista Part 3	Filing Fundamentals	1-933404-71-X
DVD	The Internet IE7 Part 1	Searching the Internet	1-933404-68-X
DVD	E-mail Windows Mail Part 1	The Basics	1-933404-69-8
DVD	Word 2007 Part 1	An Introduction to Word Processing	1-933404-72-8
DVD	Excel 2007 Part 1	An Introduction to Spreadsheets	1-933404-73-6
DVDs are $19.95 each.			
To Order Call Toll Free: 1-866-232-7032			